**THE MOST SHOCKING, MOST GRUESOME
BOOK OF THE YEAR!
READ ABOUT
THE SAILOR WHO DIED FROM THE PRICK
OF A BLUE OCTOPUS**

* * *

**THE BOY WHO WAS DEVOURED BY AN
ALLIGATOR IN THE CARANAJOE SWAMP**

* * *

**THE REPORTER WHO DIED IN AGONY
AFTER A CANDIRU ENTERED HIS BODY**

* * *

**THE CHILD WHO WAS INSTANTLY
PARALYZED AFTER THE STING OF THE
INVISIBLE SEA WASP!**

* * *

**THE ACTRESS WHO WAS DEVOURED
BY A GREAT WHITE SHARK**

* * *

**THE DIVER WHO WAS ATTACKED
BY A SEA SNAKE, AND HIS SLOW,
TORTUROUS DEATH**

* * *

**PLUS, MANY, MANY MORE—
INCLUDING DARING, SHOCKING PHOTOS**

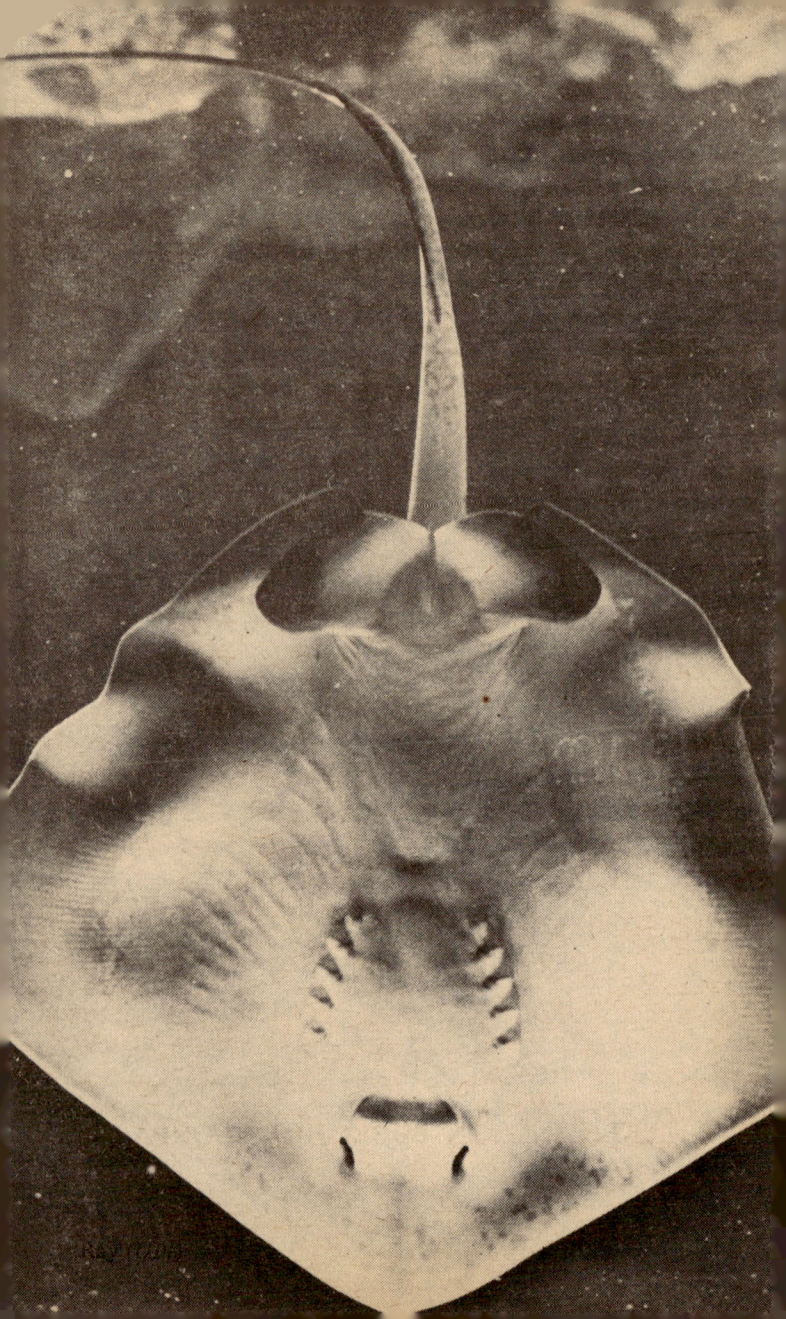

SEA KILLERS

By Jim Wyckoff

ZEBRA BOOKS

KENSINGTON PUBLISHING CORP.

ZEBRA BOOKS
are published by
KENSINGTON PUBLISHING CORP.
380 Madison Avenue
New York, N.Y. 10017

Copyright © 1975 by KENSINGTON PUBLISHING CORP.

All rights reserved. No part of this book may be reproduced in any form or by any means without the prior written consent of the Publisher, excepting brief quotes used in reviews.

First Printing: December, 1975

Printed in the United States of America

FOREWORD

Do sea serpents actually exist? Are there such beings as the mythological monsters of the deep? Since the dawn of history man has been fascinated with this question. Beyond all the efforts of orthodox science to explain away the notion of sea monsters attacking men and ships, the belief persists. For it is a fact that the sea serpents are there.

Killers of the sea not only exist, they have been seen, and they do attack human beings. Many of them have been photographed, though by no means all of them. And some have been captured.

Without question the abiding connection in all cases of attack by any of these underwater denizens is the fact of violence — and also terror. One is frightened, to be sure, by the prospect of a charge by a mad bear, a berserk gorilla, a lion, or a condor swooping down with claws outstretched and beak dripping, but for some reason the beasts of the sea — including those equally ferocious inhabitants of lake, river, lagoon, and swamp — are infinitely more terrifying.

That this is so can be swiftly attested to by one's own reaction upon hearing or reading of the effects of an attack by the great white shark, the giant squid, the piranha, the alligator gar, or the killer whale. The mangled remains — or simply instant skeleton — of the victims are more chillingly eloquent than any words.

The point is that these terrors of the deep are not only silent but they are invisible. One can find a certain sort of "security" in being able to see a charging rhino, or a crazed tiger, but a shark, a giant sting ray, a stonefish, a barracuda, are unseen, silent, swift — and their visit upon the victim is more often than not wholly irrevocable, while their imprint on our imaginations has the shattering blast of an earthquake.

They are not seen, these monsters until the moment they rise up from the deep. Even worse — as in the case of the great shark's dorsal fin — they may be partially seen. And even then it is very often too late.

It is undoubtedly their mystery that is so frightful. No one really knows where one of them will strike. Or why. Or when. And moreover — unimaginable terror — we are not sure if the attacker is even known, or if it is some new or ancient, prehistoric species of monster like the fabled Kraker, or giant squid who in 1875 took a ship full of men to the bottom.

For who really knows what lives beneath the water? Is there perhaps a bigger, even more terrifying, shark than the one that terrorized the New Jersey beaches in 1916, killing four swimmers? Are there other monsters down there, serpents who may only now begin to appear, perhaps driven to the surface or to shallower waters as a result of geological changes or by the pollution of oceans and rivers? The legends of the monster of Loch Ness and the monster of Loch Morar are not founded in fantasy.

Over the centuries these underwater beings with their sinuous movements, their enormous jaws and claws of steel, their poisons and their fantastic strength and rapacity have gripped man with awe and terror.

And it is beside the point to argue whether a certain animal attacks only through a misunderstanding or from fear or from reprisal; the grim fact is that it does attack, and it is of small consequence for what reason when an arm or leg has been savaged from a person's body or he has been crushed like an eggshell, or cut to pieces in a matter of seconds, or dies an agonizing, lingering death from an unassailable venom. The monsters are there. Perhaps the best thing we can do is respect them.

THE TWELVE DAY HORROR THAT NOBODY CAN FORGET

It was sixty years ago that the great white shark stalked the New Jersey coast, killing four people.

The sun-baked beach was packed with bathers, all happy over the approaching Fourth of July celebration, which would be in two days. Children ran in and out of the water, splashing one another: the smaller ones built their castles in the sand. The young men courted the young girls, and the older couples soaked in the life-giving salt air.

In Europe there was the war, for this was 1916, but here at Beach Haven, New Jersey, it was holiday time. There wasn't a soul on the beach or in the delightfully cool water who could know that the most unforgettable horror was about to strike.

No one saw the great white beast moving stealthily through the silent water about 100 meters from the laughing shore. No ripple, no sound, not the slightest vibration heralded his arrival on a joyous scene that in only seconds would turn to unimaginable havoc.

Charles Vanzant, a handsome young man of twenty-four, turned in the cool, placid sea and began to swim leisurely back to the beach. He was hungry. He would have one of those great hot dogs and a beer, then perhaps a gentle snooze under the sun. He was really developing a tan. The girls at the office...

He swam on his back now and his ears were in the water and so he did not hear the great scream that rose from the crowds on the beach.

In total horror they followed an old man's pointing finger to the fin that had broken the surface just a few feet from Vanzant, and his near-scream, "SHARK!"

And the cry went up, almost sobbing out of the staring crowd, "My God — *it is a shark!*"

Charles Vanzant heard nothing. His head was in the water. He was thinking how his tan would impress the girls at the office when he returned to work.

The great white shark swam closer. The dorsal fin sliced the surface of the water like a razor.

Vanzant, swimming on his back, had closed his eyes against the heat of the July sun. He felt a pull on his leg. Still without opening his eyes he reached down, thinking he might have swum into a fishing net or a rope of some kind. He could not find his leg. When he opened his eyes he saw the great fin and the blood foaming to the surface, pumping out of the hole where his leg had once been a part of his body. He screamed. And he kept on screaming....

There are still eyewitnesses to that scene of unbelievable horror. They remember that day sixty years ago. An eyewitness recollected it only recently.

"There was a lot of churning in the water when Vanzant began flailing his arms and screaming.

"Then the water turned red, foaming, like it was boiling or something. A bunch of us rushed in to help.

"Maybe the noise we made or the crashing in the water — I don't know — but anyhow the shark took off. We grabbed Vanzant and got him to the beach. The sea was all blood. My God, I've never seen so much blood. And I have never seen anything like what was left of his legs. I think one was completely gone, the other was like shredded meat. But — blood... My God, blood all over..."

Charles Vanzant never did show his tan to the girls in the office. He died from loss of blood and shock. His legs and body had been totally ravaged by the great fanged beast.

But this was only the beginning of an orgy of destruction that left mangled bodies, an ocean of human blood, and terror, sheer terror, in the hearts and minds of those who were fortunate enough to survive.

Except nobody knew that it was only the beginning; everyone though it was over. The funeral was held. The family mourned. The holiday-makers were in no mood for a holiday now. They retreated into their sorrow and shrinking memories of the horror they had witnessed at Beach Haven. It was more than enough for a lifetime.

But just four days later the great killer struck again! Forty-five miles up the coast, at Spring Lake, New Jersey, twenty-eight-year-old Charlie

Pruder (also listed as Bruder, age twenty-three) was enjoying the cool water and a vigorous swim. He was a good swimmer, strong, and sure of himself in the water. As was his custom he was swimming well beyond the lifeline. But nobody paid much notice, for they knew his capabilities. He could handle himself.

A young woman on the beach was idly watching him, watching rather in the way one will casually notice birds or an airplane, not really taking it in, for one's attention is actually on something else.

Suddenly she saw that Pruder had disappeared — and that where he had been swimming a spreading red blot appeared.

The woman screamed. Pointing, she cried out that the man in the red canoe had turned over and must be in trouble.

But it was no "canoe." It was the great white shark she had seen, and now to the horrified eyes of all on the beach there was no question what the "red" was.

Pruder had been swimming along at a good clip. He loved to swim. His body was strong, well-knit, he loved to move it. Swimming was one of his favorite pastimes.

He wondered if he had gotten off his course and had run into the lifeline, for he felt a tug. But then, to his unimaginable horror, *he knew...*

Lifeguards quickly reached Pruder by boat. They reached over to pull him aboard.

Just before he lost consciousness in a haze of agony, he gasped, "Shark — shark got me — bit my legs off!"

Death was quick. Mercifully so. Pruder's right leg was in shreds, that is, what was left of it. It was bitten off halfway between the knee and ankle, residing now in the great belly of his attacker along with the left foot and lower part of the left leg which were also missing. Most of the remaining left leg below the knee was totally denuded of flesh, and there was a deep gash above the left knee. As though this "feast" had not been sufficient, the terrible teeth had savaged out a large mouthful from the right side of his victim's abdomen.

Where now was the killer? And was it one killer? Or a group? By now the entire coast was in a state of alarm. And there was more to come.

And it came in a most unexpected manner — not that anyone ever "expects" a shark attack. But in many ways, this one may be termed the most tragic of the attacks. It happened six days later.

Matawan, New Jersey is about twenty-five miles from where Charles Pruder had been killed. Actually, Matawan is some ten miles from the ocean; its connection is a tidal creek, about 35 feet across at its widest point, and which runs about two miles before emptying into Raritan Bay.

The afternoon of July 12 was uncomfortable; it was hot, muggy, a harbinger of the dog days that would come in August. A group of boys knew how to deal with that sort of weather, though. They were enjoying themselves in the cool waters of their favorite swimming hole in Matawan Creek.

Earlier that same day three men on a bridge about a mile and half down stream had seen a dark shadow sweeping up the creek with the incoming tide, and heading straight as an arrow for Matawan.

Could it be a shark? Their warnings were not taken seriously, though, because who would ever think of a shark finding its way up that narrow stream, so far from the open sea? Why would a shark even think of coming up there?

At any rate, the happy swimmers diving from the piling near a makeshift dock in front of the bag factory at Matawan never gave it a thought.

The water was murky, and now one of the boys who drove in felt something rough grate across his stomach. Rocks? He clambered out of the water quickly.

"Don't dive in any more — there's a shark or something in there!" And he looked at his stomach to see it streaked with blood.

What had he scraped against?

"There are no sharks this far up the creek," someone said. "You scraped on a rock or some old wood or nail or something."

Soon they were all caught up in a game of tag. The warning was forgotten, even by the boy who had scraped his stomach.

Presently, twelve-year-old Lester Stilwell called to a friend who was just climbing out of the water.

"Watch me float!"

As the other boy turned to watch Lester, he felt something slam against his leg. Looking down, he saw what he thought was the tail of a huge fish. And all at once he was gripped with fear. It was heading straight for his friend Lester. But before he could cry out in warning, the great beast was upon his victim.

Lester of course had seen nothing, for he was floating on his back. His scream of terror coincided almost to the dot with the bite of the monster whose great teeth but almost all the way through him. The poor boy was pulled down into the murky depths.

Instant terror boke out. People suddenly appeared at the creek, would-be rescuers and others who attempted to calm the screaming boys. Some people were in boats, others, not realizing what was happening, only thinking that one of the boys was drowning, dove into the water. It was wholly courageous but foolhardy as the whole group became submered in utter hysteria.

Meanwhile, the water foamed with the struggle that was going on beneath. Now the entire creek, it seemed, had exploded into bright red. This did not deter Stanley Fisher who rushed into the water to help some other men who were attempting to block the shark's escape by stretching a chicken-wire barrier across a narrow place downstream from where Lester Stilwell had disappeared.

Fisher was a big man, about 240 pounds, in his early twenties. Now he bravely began diving to try to find the boy's body.

And then, as onlookers watched, a shout went up, for a great shadow could be seen in the water, bearing down upon Fisher. Some onlookers later estimated it at fifteen feet in length. All at once the water around Fisher began to boil, as the shark bit with his enormous jaws. The creek seemed to whip into a gigantic crimson foam. The man disappeared. He was heroically battling the shark with every ounce he could muster — hitting, kicking, biting; his entire being screaming at the rage and terror of it.

Meanwhile, on the surface, the water churned even more violently and grew a brighter red. For a moment the onlookers were paralyzed by this second horror, unbelievable in its suddenness.

But now Fisher was seen to surface in a great stain of new blood. The water was waist-deep and he was half crouching, tottering on one leg while holding the remains of his right leg in both hands.

This horrific sight stunned the onlookers, most of whom simply could not believe what they were seeing. The flesh had been stripped from Fisher's right thigh, from his groin to his knee. The white, bloodstreaked thigh bone was clearly visible through the torn and bloody flesh.

As the brave man — his face absolutely disfigured by the pain and shock of what he was suffering — began to fall, hands reached out from a boat which had been swiftly manned, and grabbed him.

In vain they tried to stop the bleeding by putting a rope tourniquet high on the thigh. The courageous man died that night in the hospital, but he was able to state that he had actually reached the body of Lester Stilwell and had wrested it from the jaws of the shark. It was reported that the body of the boy was found two days later not very far from where Fisher had been cut to pieces.

But the horror was not over; the orgy of blood and terror and torment was to continue almost without any interruption. Some men had decided to get dynamite and blow up the hiding killer.

They would dynamite the creek. And while this was being done, and even while Fisher was being rushed to the hospital, the great white shark struck again. This time about a half mile downstream.

Joseph Dunn and several other boys were swimming in the creek when the shark warning reached them. They heeded it. They scrambled out of the water. But Joseph Dunn was the last to climb into the motor boat.

Just as he was about to clear the water the white killer bit into his right leg. The boy turned white, screamed and kicked the water with his free leg while his friends tried to pull him from the shark's jaws.

Meanwhile the wretched boy was screaming and kicking, his face a grotesque mask of unspeakable pain and panic.

But finally they managed to wrench Dunn free of those massive teeth which sliced with the speed of light, the precision of the professional killer, and the inexorability of death.

The brute now vanished. Onlookers testified that he was a good twelve or fifteen feet in length. It was hard to see in the murky water, and everyone was so horrified and afraid too that no doubt they saw more through imagination than cool scientific observation.

Joseph Dunn recovered, although it was necessary to amputate his leg.

The great white shark escaped, crashing through the chicken-wire barrier and vanishing. At least for the moment. Hundreds of nets, baited hooks and other articles of capture failed to get him.

Great white shark, weighing 1,400 pounds, measuring 12½ feet long. *(UPI)*

While one account says that Lester Stilwell's body was found (as noted above) another account says that "it is believed that the child was literally torn to pieces and devoured."

A massive shark hunt was mounted, with the entire countryside roused. A number of sharks were caught in and near Matawan Creek. It is supposed that the actual assassin was an 8½-foot great white shark which was netted in Raritan Bay, less than four miles from the mouth of the creek. This was two days after the holocaust. When they opened the killer they found in its belly fifteen pounds of human flesh and bones, including those identified as the shinbone of a boy and part of a human rib cage.

The authorities were satisfied that this one had been the killer, for there were no more attacks.

There is no doubt that the great white shark attacks more humans than any other kind of shark. Clearly, it is the most dangerous of its tribe. Furthermore, it grows to an astounding size, which alone is sufficient to strike terror into anyone. Often the great white shark exceeds twenty feet. One great white shark caught off the Australian coast measured more than thirty-six feet.

These brutes are also solidly built. In 1959, also in Australian waters, a 16½-foot white shark weighed in at 2,664 pounds; a twenty-one-footer, hooked off Cuba, is said to have tipped the beam at seven thousand pounds.

They often swallow their prey whole. Their teeth

are triangular and saw-edged and so it's an easy matter to chew off a piece of the victim. But they can take a big gulp. One great white shark, measuring thirty feet, taken off the coast of California, was found to have a hundred-pound sea lion in its stomach.

Big, or not so big, they are deadly, rapacious, and fearsome. That infamous day at Matawan has not been forgotten. Nor will it be.

THE TRUE SEA SERPENT

"Marlboro country it is not," Don Widdicomb said as he eased his forty-foot steel-hulled *Baby Doe* into the shelter of a reef.

We were a long way from home, John Farkas and I. We had traveled twenty-seven flying hours from New York to Sydney, and then had sailed on up some two-hundred miles north to Australia's Great Barrier Reef.

A long way out here, I remember I was thinking as I looked at that impassive, and so seemingly peaceful sea...and a long way back. Right then I didn't have any idea how really long that return trip was going to be.

Of course, Don was referring to the "country" below the surface. "Snake country," the anglers call it. John and I had come to this remote region of bursting surf and treacherous shoals and placid, clear sea to observe and photograph snakes underwater.

Few divers had ever done this, and not many

scientists. First of all, the sea snakes we were after are thousands of miles "away"; that is, they don't live in the Atlantic.

They probably would, scientists claim, but for the narrow neck of the isthmus of Panama. They cannot cross the isthmus through the Panama Canal because the freshwater lakes in the canals do not allow the passage of marine life from one ocean to the other. As a matter of fact, if sea snakes ever should enter fresh water, they would lose necessary amounts of body salts and die.

The freshwater barrier that is provided by the Panama Canal would be lacking if there happened to be a sea-level canal across the isthmus; and a sea snake invasion from the Pacific to the Atlantic is one of the most dreaded consequences of such a project. Not only would an invasion of sea snakes into the Atlantic drive tourists out of the Caribbean and cut off the flow of money in trade, but it would have a most serious effect on the ecological balance.

Sea snakes have been known since remote times. As a rule these serpents of the sea remain near the shore, but they have been seen in great numbers, even covering the surface, on the open sea. One such armada, sixty miles long and ten feet wide was sighted in 1932 between Sumatra and the Malay Peninsula. Within that massive, awesome horde of venom millions of serpentine bodies, stroking and undulating with their wicked-looking flat tails, surged on, no one knew to where. It must have been a horrific sight — for their bite is agonizingly lethal.

John and I wanted to study the feeding and mating habits and especially the behavior toward people of these dangerous creatures. We had heard some pretty rough stories and were intrigued, although, speaking for myself right now, I wouldn't have wanted to go alone or with anyone I didn't know as well as John Farkas. John was a true pro when it came to this sort of work. The only thing was, though both of us had been diving for years, we didn't know much at all about these creatures.

I want to say here that I had never believed in sea serpents or sea monsters and all those gory stories, but I was soon to change my mind. Abruptly.

Don Widdicomb, whose boat we'd hired, told us right off we were crazy.

"You don't know what one of them can do to you," was how he put it. "I mean, a single shark bite, all right, it's nothing to look forward to, but you've still got a chance. But when old *Pelamus platurus* or *A. stokesii* sink one of those fangs into you — just one nibble — you have had it." He shook his big head, whistling through his teeth. "I saw an Aborigine fisherman get it last year. I watched him die. It's not a sight to remember at night."

We knew Don was right, but we were determined. A great many humans had already died from being bitten by sea snakes. Some of these serpents — and there are about fifty varieties — have a venom many times more deadly than that known for any land snake. The particular one we were after was a member of the *Hydrophiidae* family, cousin of the cobra. Just remembering what happened now, all this time later, I can sense that feeling so many writers have described, and **which until now I always thought was the bunk —** the hair rising on the back of my neck. These deadly vipers can go to eight feet in length, but long or short they *all have those fangs.*

But diving is like anything else; once you're hooked, you're hooked.

The area we were in was excellent for our purpose. The water was absolutely clear. You could see all the way to the bottom in some places.

That first day was unforgettable, not only because it was our first dive — but because of the superbly beautiful setting. The water was as clear, as blue, and in many places as tranquil, as the great sky overhead.

I couldn't wait to get into the water. That first moment when you slip over the side of the boat and the water closes over your head is always special for me. I knew it was special for John too, for we had sometimes spoken of it. As I have said, we were old diving buddies. And that feeling of excitement, of newness, of a whole world opening up, well, it's especially so when you're in a new region, one that no one else, or hardly anyone, has explored.

I never expected it to happen so fast. I really wasn't ready and the chill that went through me in that warm water almost paralyzed me.

A sort of motion, a sinuous curving on the sand floor of the sea. Even though the setting seemed almost more like the interior of a fish tank than the actual sea I felt that chill of fear, of the unknown, go all the way through me. It's a fear I think that men have known ever since the beginning of time — the fear of the serpent.

I've been diving for years, nearly all my life, and I was long familiar with the abrupt darting and searching of numerous kinds of fish. But this, this was that all-too-familiar motion of the silent, venomous — and unknown — serpent that has evoked fascination and terror in man ever since the beginning of history.

I was prepared, at least externally. My insides were shaky, but I had my snake stick, an aluminum rod with a pistol grip on one end and tonglike jaws on the other; about the length of a rifle. And I was — luckily — covered completely by my diving suit of foam rubber, which gave me protection not only against the July cold of Australian winter but, hopefully too, against the chance of snakebite. I only hoped that the snake confronting me now was the shorter-fanged species. At least one sea snake, *Astrotia,* can knife his fangs through quarter-inch neoprene foam.

He was aiming at me right now. His unmarked mustard yellow skin seemed just another variation of the water. But I recognized his kind — *Aipysurus laevis* — which can reach better than six feet in length. And I now saw he was indeed all of that.

He had a heavy body and a mouth big enough for serious biting. His head was like a cobra's, neat and

24

blunt, and he had the cobra's large, dark — and I am tempted to say baleful — eye. The absolutely incongruous thing was that his face appeared actually pleasant. He even seemed to offer a small smile. But then crocodiles and their "gently smiling jaws" also appear pleasant. Until they stop smiling!

This is not a moment I care to remember; still it was nothing compared to what happened the following day. I have often wondered, though, whether or not it might have been some sort of warning or premonition.

As he swam closer, just about six inches from my stomach, I could feel myself tighten, even sweat. Would those fangs strike? How long were they? Would they pierce my suit? I knew that the strike would be painless; and I might not even feel it. It would be later that the torture of its poison would **seize the body and cause excruciating death. And just one strike was enough.**

His kind had killed a lot of people. As I said, the bite is painless. But after several hours the legs of the victim become paralyzed, his eyes close, and then his jaws lock. He may live for several days before convulsions and respiratory failure bring longed-for death. All these gruesome thoughts were racing in me as that awesome figure slid closer.

But no — his jaws remained serenely closed and he swam on, almost brushing me. So much for my first encounter with a true sea serpent.

It was the next morning that it happened — but, of course, not in any way that I could possibly have expected.

Again it was a magnificent day. The three of us

had slept well after Don had served a delicious supper of snapper, salad, and garlic bread, with superb wine. The Australian wines are little known in the rest of the world, but a number of them are delicious, rivaling anything I've had in France or Germany or back in the States.

We had spent the rest of the evening swapping stories and sitting in silence too under the massive, fabulous sky, the myriad stars, and of course, the southern cross. We were tired in that marvelously honest way one can be after a great day, but we were loath to turn in. I was still a bit shaken, too, by my encounter with that mustard-colored devil.

"Tomorrow we'll get some really good specimens for the lab," John said eagerly. He had sighted a couple of snakes, but he had not had an experience like mine, and so he had kidded me a good bit.

"Just be careful when they come up for air," Don warned. "It's the worst time. That's when they notice you, and sometimes they'll just come right at you."

"And attack?"

"If that's what you call having those poisonous fangs hit you, yes," said Don in his laconic way.

I remembered Don's admonition as I got ready the following morning. We were in a new region now and when I slipped over the side I told myself I was ready for any fresh surprises.

Again, I saw my adversary almost immediately. This was a different sea serpent who came undulating into my field of vision. He was small, only a couple of feet long, and, in spite of again feeling

Laticauda colubrina—common-banded sea snake *(New York Zoological Society Photo)*

that tug of fear, I could say he was beautiful, with his belly a smooth yellow. I knew that *Pelamus platurus* was highly poisonous and that he could swim with unbelievable speed. This is because he can fold his skin to form a deep, flattened ventral keel. He can swim so fast that he seems to just disappear. What was he going to do now?

I kept more or less still, with my eyes watching him, as though mesmerized. But then, with total unexpectedness, another figure appeared on the scene.

A long body as thick as my arm, a body that seemed to glitter, a pale body, though with dark patterns. His face, I quickly saw, unlike my friend of the previous day, was not smiling.

Somehow, *Pelamus platurus* had left my field of vision, and this rather frightened me. Still, the serpent in front of me now was bearing down, and there was no time to look around for the other. And it was definitely time for action.

I caught him with my snake stick well back along his body. Too far back! He turned instantly, like light, snapping viciously as he did so. And now he immediately began sliding back toward my hand that was holding the stick.

I realized with a stab of horror that the jaws of my snake stick would not hold him. And where was *Pelamus platurus*? But I didn't have time to give in to my fear, thank heaven for that. It was all happening too quickly for panic to set in. But in a moment, feeling the serpent force on my snake stick, I really touched my terror and I almost did give in to panic. I wanted to drop snake and snake stick and just get out of there. But I would have been a goner. He would have got me and no question.

Instead I grabbed with my left hand at a point just behind that pink, gaping, angry mouth. And I held on. I just prayed that my foam rubber gloves would protect me if he got in a strike.

It was all I could do to hold him, especially as I was trying to see the other snake. Had he left? Or would the furor of the battle bring him in for a strike?

He was strong! He swiftly threw coils around my arm and got ready to bite if I should loosen my grip. I was really locked onto him. Fear gave me a strength and determination I had never known before.

But where was the boat? Further away than I had thought, as I realized with a great thrust of alarm. Now I tried to hurry toward it. My arm ached. I had trouble moving it seemed. Where was the boat! Had it drifted? Where were John and Don; I cursed myself for not staying closer to them.

It seemed an interminable time before I saw the boat. I tried to tighten my grip on the snake, for I was terrified that my grip would loosen without my realizing it, and it would be too late.

Somehow I crawled up the ladder with my furious adversary, and with one final effort I blindly flipped Mr. Snake into a wet bag that was on the deck.

Then I sat down.

John came aboard to look at my catch. It was Don, though, who recognized the snake.

"Congratulations," he said with a big grin. "That nice little fellow is known as *Astrotia stokesii*. He's rare in these parts, and he's a big one."

I rubbed my arms and stretched my cramped fingers. "He was big all right." I suddenly felt damn tired.

John said, "He was really trying to bite you."

"You're a lucky boy," Don said. "You know, he can go right through those gloves."

"There was another one down there," I said, and

I told them about *Pelamus platurus*.

Don chuckled. "Like I said, you're a lucky diver."

I was shaking, I realized then. But I didn't want to show it, so I forced a grin. It must have looked pretty ghastly. I looked at the sack, and at my gloves. Thank God I had held my grip; or maybe that "something," some power someplace, had held it for me.

"We'll stick closer together from now on," John said. "It was my fault. I got hung up on some pictures."

"I could use a small drink," I said suddenly, feeling myself go weak all over as I recalled those eyes that bore down on me, and saw again the inside of that yawning, furious, silken mouth with its fangs that were only waiting to kill me.

This remark brought a burst of laughter from the two of them. And I began to laugh too. I guess it all helped loosen me.

But suddenly John left out a small cry, the kind of surprised cry one gives on being unexpectedly hit, though not very painfully.

I turned my head to look at him and saw to my unbelievable horror that *A. stokesii* was out of the bag. Without a moment's thought I picked up a two-by-four that was lying by my feet and brought it down on that ugly head. One blow was enough. Still, I was too late.

"I think he hit me," John said in the calmest voice I have ever heard in my life.

"I've got antivenin," Don said quietly, and he ran to the cabin of the small craft.

John had turned white under his tan. The fang marks were clear on the foot as I slashed into them with my knife and began to suck out the poison.

Don was there with the antivenin, though all three of us knew it was useless. There is no known serum for any of the reef snakes. But he tried it. We would have tried anything.

"I'm feeling no pain at all," John said calmly as we tried to get all possible speed out of the *Baby Doe*. Yet, I knew he was scared. Who wouldn't have been? You're not supposed to feel anything for a while, as we all knew. No pain, but then paralysis, the eyes close, the jaws lock, then convulsions, respiratory blocking, agony — until the arrival of death.

John knew this, and I could read it in his eyes. I tried to talk about other things, but I must have been speaking a lot of gibberish.

It was the longest journey I've ever taken. I kept trying to get John's thoughts away from the snake. But I knew I was failing. Finally, it began to hit him. There's a point, I think, up to which you can fight off certain fears, and then you can't anymore. But how high is your threshold when you've been fanged by the most dangerous sea snake, and you *know* nothing will help?

Our only chance was that I had slashed soon enough and gotten the poison out, or at least some of it. Although I asked myself what I meant by "some." Just a drop of that venom could kill a man.

Don was "talking" the boat into port with everything he could muster; praying, swearing, begging it to move faster. I think I was more terrified than either he or John. We were about another twenty minutes out of port when it got to poor John. I could see the shock taking over. His face became dead white, ashen, and he seemed to have trouble breathing. He was trying to rub his arms.

And suddenly his eyes closed! I knew then we'd had it. I swore. I looked at Don. He was staring wildly at John. "Pray!" he called out to me. "Pray — with all you've got!"

And I did.

I hardly remember docking or getting John ashore. Thank God there were people. We rushed him to the hospital. He was already in convulsions, his arms jerking, his face a mask of unbelievable agony. He kept trying to speak, and I knew he was bravely trying to control his terror. But I could see it in his eyes, which were suddenly brilliant with a fear as sharp as that damned snake fang.

The doctors worked on him. They pumped his stomach, gave him artificial respiration, massaged his limbs.

The terrible thing I remember was that when John tried to speak the most horrendous sound came from him — a cry that was the most inhuman thing I have ever heard. I don't know what he was trying to say — if anything, really. Maybe he was asking for the end. Who can say.

And maybe I shouldn't say this, but after spending hours upon hours with my friend I wanted the end to come. For him. I asked myself how much agony and terror a human being could be asked to take. For John was no longer John, no longer a human being. He had become a "thing," a wretched vessel for terror, unbelievable suffering, and, finally, an excruciating death.

SWAMP KILLER

There is that famous saying that "Life is really a grade B movie." Maybe it is. But there are times when life becomes, for a while at least, a horror movie.

It was surely this way one spring afternoon in Carahanjoe Swamp. So horrible an event transpired that I have changed the names of the participants, and the actual place, for the protection of the privacy of those involved. It is no pleasure to be reminded again and again of past tragedies by prying and inquisitive people, no matter how decent their motives.

It was a balmy day, May 24, 1962, when two boys — Charles and Terry Morris — played hooky from school and went adventuring into the great swamp. As is so often the case, the boys — age twelve and ten, respectively — had been warned by their parents against entering the swamp on their own. But also, like so many adventurous boys, they had ignored the warning.

The day was delightfully warm. The boys were excited; as one of them reported later, they hoped to meet some real Indians. They'd "had enough school for a day," was how Terry, the tow-headed ten-year-old, put it.

It did occur to them that they should be careful; still, that was obviously a secondary consideration.

The Morris family had only recently moved to Carahanjoe, which is not very far from New Orleans. They were originally from Ohio, but Fred Morris' business had sent him south to help open a new branch. The family of four had been in Carahanjoe just a year.

Fred Morris was at work when the telephone call came. It was from Betty, his wife, reporting that the school had called to say that neither Charles nor Terry had shown up that morning. Betty Morris had control of the alarm behind her voice, yet it was audible to her sensitive husband.

He told her not to worry, the boys had probably decided to be adventurous and play hooky. Still, it wasn't usual for them, he reflected as he hung up the receiver.

Fred Morris then telephoned the local police, and he left his office early that day. When he got home he found a distraught wife and no news of the children. It was when their grade teacher appeared that the Morrises learned that one of the other children had reported having heard Charles and Terry mentioning their plan to "one day go see the Indians in Carahanjoe Swamp."

"Oh my God," said Fred Morris, and he grabbed

the telephone.

His wife stared wildly at the clock on the kitchen wall. It was 4:30 in the afternoon. Just then they heard a car draw up outside the house and when both of them reached the front door they were met by two policemen.

Hardly a word was spoken as the Morrises were driven to the local hospital where they found their youngest son Terry in bed in a state of shock, with one arm swathed in bandages, and with other bandages on his face and legs.

"He may lose that arm," the doctor in attendance informed them. "There's a fifty-fifty chance."

The boy's parents stared in horror as they listened to the doctor and the police report.

"The arm is — well, it's pretty much shredded."

"But — how?" Fred Morris could hardly get the words out.

It was the police lieutenant who spoke now. "As far as we can tell at this point, Mr. Morris, it was an alligator." He paused, running his tongue over his dry lips. "Your other boy..."

He didn't finish. The Morrises were beyond hearing what they must have already known by now.

Carahanjoe Swamp is one of the most mysterious places in the United States. There are still parts of it that remain uncharted. It is a real forest, mostly underwater, marvelously picturesque, but also filled with unknown dangers. Even the Indians are careful here. The whites are not sure just what animals do inhabit the swamp, although they have checked out quite a few. Carahanjoe Swamp is a place of great fascination, but it is the fascination of fear, of the devil. There are strange and terrifying noises and it is extraordinarily easy to get lost. The countryside is filled with tales of people disappearing in the swamp. Indeed, there is a saying when someone has not been around socially for a while that he or she "must have gotten into Carahanjoe." And children, of course, have always frightened each other and themselves with horror tales of the great swamp, brimming with venomous snakes, crocodiles and giant alligators, and maybe even giant reptiles left over from the age of dinosaurs.

Not very long before Charles and Terry had their adventure a young man got lost in Carahanjoe. He was found three days after he had been seen entering the swamp, his mind gone, babbling, his eyes staring as though locked on some unbelievable horror. He had been taken to the hospital, but before he could even be put to bed he had gone into severe shock and died.

Terry Morris's arm was amputated at the shoulder, and he eventually recovered. But he could remember nothing of what happened. He had no idea how long he was in the swamp, how long it took him to get out, or how; and he had no memory of the police finding him. When asked about his brother Charles, he simply looked blank and wanted to know where Charles was.

Finally, and with the permission of his parents, the doctors administered sodium **pentothal.** Even this didn't appear at first to jog the boy's memory, but on the third try they were successful; and eventually the whole story came out. At last Fred and Betty Morris learned the horrifying details of what had happened to their sons in Carahanjoe Swamp.

Anyone who has been through the experience knows how terribly difficult it is to get a story out of someone who has undergone some terrifying event, especially a child. It takes inordinate patience, care in leading the conversation and, above all, concern for the one who is telling what happened.

But the drug was what did it. And the doctors were good at their work. Sodium pentothal, known as the "truth drug," really brought Terry back into the terrible events that had happened. But it also brought him into a realistic replay, so that the poor boy went through the whole thing again, as though he was actually there. It was a shattering experience not only for him but for his distraught parents, and for the doctors as well.

The boys had entered the swamp in a happy mood. Theirs was a feeling of adventure, spiced too by the fact that they had cut school. They rationalized this a bit by telling themselves they would be doing research for their classes in biology and also American history; after all, they were bound to see some animals along the way to their hoped-for encounter with Indians.

They followed the trail that first presented itself to them, moving along swiftly in the morning sunlight, which shortly began to fade as they drew further into the great swamp.

The boys were thrilled. They passed all sorts of birds, beautiful flowers and plants, all the while to the sounds of myriad animals singing.

"Boy, I sure wouldn't want to spend th... out here," Charles said, looking up at the sky, far and dim above the moss-hung trees.

They kept right on the trail, mindful of the dangers they had heard about travelers getting lost, and watching closely for snakes.

At noontime, more or less, they stopped for lunch. Both were ravenously hungry and so they sat down in a small clearing and had their sandwiches, cokes and candy bars. They were there probably half an hour. They then pressed further into the swamp, wondering when they would come upon some Indians.

Perhaps another hour passed. Terry was not too clear about the actual length of time, for they had no watch with them. But at a certain place along the trail, where it appeared to double back on the other side of a fairly narrow inlet, they decided to return. They had met no Indians and were disappointed. But, as Charles pointed out, the light was going and it was obviously getting late.

It was Charles's suggestion that, rather than take the longer way and double back on the trail to the other side, that they would ford the inlet.

"But we don't know if that trail will lead us back," Terry said.

"But we can try it," Charles insisted. "Go along for a few yards and see if it does or not. And if it doesn't, we'll come back."

Terry was still doubtful. "I want to get on back," he said, and his tone was not happy.

"..ook," said Charles. He was always the leader, probably because of being older. "We can jump across on those rocks and logs. It'll only take a minute."

"No. Come on," Terry said. But he knew he was not going to convince his brother.

"You wait here," Charles said. "I'll just take a look over there."

And, without waiting for Terry to answer him, he started over the narrow body of water, stepping on a rock, then a log, and another rock....

Terry saw — or thought he saw — the log move. But it was too late even to call out; the words died in his throat.

Charles screamed as the alligator rose and he went hurtling into the swamp. All Terry could see was a churning mass of water and arms and legs, and then — horror of horrors — those great jaws with the sabre-sharp teeth. And then the swamp was suddenly crimson. Charles was screaming. And now as Terry looked he saw his brother trapped right in the alligator's massive jaws. Those tremendous teeth were snapped shut, cutting the poor boy almost in two. For a flash the beast seemed to shake its head, then gripping Charles's mangled, bloodsoaked body he disappeared beneath the red water.

Terry was screaming at the top of his lungs. Somehow he had found a fallen branch and was wildly beating the water with it. Now, other "logs" began to churn in the swamp; or perhaps they had already been moving and he had not noticed. One great jaw seized the end of the branch and with a tremendous jerk the boy was pulled into the water. He screamed again, trying to drag himself up onto firm land by grabbing a small tree. But the tree came out by the roots.

Suddenly he felt a thump on his arm. Now he got a better hold on another tree and pulled himself out of the water, just as the bloodstreaked jaws of the great alligator snapped behind him.

He lay on the ground, panting, sobbing, screaming, his hands and face covered with blood. But the beast was climbing up after him. Terror, sheer terror, drove the boy to his feet and he began to run. And run...

He heard a shout and something grabbed him and held him, although he fought furiously, raging and sobbing. But it was a man. An Indian. Terry had at last found the Indians he and Charles had been looking for.

When he could see again, he realized there were two men, two Indians. Then he saw the dead alligator that they had killed; an enormous, scaled beast with a tremendous mouth. Something was still in the brute's mouth, something red, and bright white. It was a piece of his brother.

The two Indians brought the hysterical boy back to town. Later, the rangers and police came to the swamp to find what was left of Charles.

The alligator gar (*Lepisosteus spatula*) is a survivor of a very ancient line of fish; indeed, he is armored like the fishes who lived before the dinosaurs. The heavy, scalelike plates that cover its body are as tough as steel, and almost as indestructible. He can grow ten feet in length, although some fishermen have claimed that certain gars grow twice that length. Charles Haskins Townsend, who was in charge of the New York Aquarium many years ago, called the alligator gar the freshwater counterpart of the shark.

The monster who attacked Charles Morris was also killed. When his abdomen was opened many human bones were found, identified as belonging to Charles. Also amongst the "findings" was a small compass given to Charles by his brother Terry on his last birthday.

It was a tragic and hideous end to young Charles Morris's life. But in a certain way perhaps it was better for Charles who died than it has been for his mother and father and for poor Terry who have had to go on living with the nightmarish memories of what happened that day in Carahanjoe.

THE TWO MINUTE-DEATH

Just because some place isn't known by a lot of people, isn't famous and doesn't "get in the news," doesn't mean that things don't happen there. Who — outside of Australia — had ever heard of Cardwell?

But maybe a few more have heard of this small town — since the events of January 1955.

It was a calm, sunny morning. This is Australia's summer, the month of January. Because they are below the equator their seasons are the opposite of ours.

The five-year-old boy was playing on the beach. His mother sat nearby, chatting with friends. It was about midway through the delightfully blue morning, and the swimmers were enjoying the beautiful beach.

"Don't go out any farther, Tommy," called the boy's mother. "He'll be a water-baby, yet," she smilingly told her friends as her proud glance fell on her only son. Patricia Hunley had the happiest of lives. A husband whom she adored and a delightful son. She was expecting a second child within a few months. Moreover, Mrs. Hunley was well-to-do and had all the friends she needed. She was successful, popular, "going somewhere" with her young husband who was in the government service.

The sky was absolutely clear; not even the suggestion of a cloud. The water was as even as a glass tabletop. Only the laughing play of happy children rang up and down the beach.

Tommy was an obedient child. He had returned from the water's edge and was now playing in shallow water six or seven feet away from the ocean.

Suddenly the air was split by his screams. He ran from the water and collapsed on the sand. His mother, paralyzed with shock for a second or two, raced from her beach chair to his side. His small body was gripped in an agonizing spasm. On his thighs and legs were the remains of what appeared to be jellyfish tentacles.

Almost beside herself with fright, the young mother began pulling off the tentacles. The skin of her young son had turned black. His face was swollen, he couldn't get his breath.

Meanwhile a crowd had gathered like lightning. Mothers were holding their children. Some men had run for medical aid, telephones, doctors. Anything! Young Tommy Hunley was in a paroxysm of pain, his face black. His young body rigid as a board. His screams tore the blue morning air.

Suddenly he fell silent. His body shook once

more, then set in its final rigidity. He was dead. Someone, for some reason or other, looked at his **wrist watch. Barely two minutes had passed since** Tommy had been bitten. Two minutes to death.

More lethal than the great white shark, silent as the sea itself, a sea wasp "hit" means death within two minutes!

And it is a death in the throes of agony: massive muscle spasms and virtual paralysis of the heart.

This terrifying, heartrending incident was typical of what had already happened to at least ninety people in North Queensland. They died from the long tentacles of *Chironex fleckeri* — the sea wasp.

This paralyzing frightful horror of the sea may grow to a length of thirty feet from tip of tentacle to the top of its "bell."

But this was not known in 1955. Until that time there had been some fifty-odd mysterious fatalities in northern Australian waters since the first recorded account seventy years before. The casual agent had never been identified, since the victim always died so quickly, and nothing abnormal was visible either above or below the surface of the water.

For years the Portuguese man-of-war *(Physalia)* had been the top suspect in these horrendous catastrophes where the wantonness and suddenness of attack and the inexorable reality of instant death had struck terror into the hearts of all who had observed them.

Following the tragedy at Cardwell, police, urged by scientists, organized an extensive search of the sea in the vicinity; as a consequence, several large box-shaped jellyfish were caught. These were kept in formalin sea water and sent to a leading authority on jelly fish, in Adelaide.

To the surprise of Dr. R. V. Southcott, the specimens did not match any previously described species. They certainly weren't Portuguese men-of-war. What were they? After Dr. Southcott's death his work was carried on, and presently *Chironex fleckeri* appeared in the scientific journals, and a new name — sea wasp — was heard.

In terms of killing velocity, the venom of the sea wasp **is one of the deadliest in the world.** *Even when diluted 10,000 times in water, it will still cause death in laboratory animals within seconds of injection.*

Dr. J.H. Barnes has described the unmistakable sign of the sea wasp when it inflicts its venom:

> During the first fifteen minutes pain increases in mounting waves, despite removal of the tentacle. The victim may scream and become irrational. Areas of contact are linear and multiple, showing as purple or brown lines often compared to the marks made by a whip. A pattern of transverse bars is usually visible. Wealing is prompt and massive. Edema, erythema and vesication soon follow, and when these subside (after some ten days), patches of full-thickness necrosis are revealed. Healing is by granulation and cicatrization, taking a month or more, and leaving permanent scars perhaps with pigment changes.

The mortality rates are difficult to estimate where this foul stinger is concerned. Not every victim succumbs; moreover, there are other jellyfish that can cause severe stinging.

Repellents are ineffective. There is an antivenin, but in view of the fact that more often than not death occurs within two minutes (and where would one get the antivenin in that short period of time), it isn't much use.

However, there is the possibility — especially now, thanks to the modern methods of resuscitation — that time may be gained so that the **wretched victim will live long enough to antivenin to be administered. Furthermore, scientists are** working on a sea wasp toxoid — a vaccine.

But this research was not very helpful to one of the more recent victims of this true monster of the sea. Mrs. Dorothy Jean Hess, age twenty-six, of Townsville, near Birsbane, Australia, was the recipient of a sea wasp sting on the second of November 1972.

The description of its effects was similar to that of Tommy Hunley. The poor woman screamed. And screamed again. Others on the beach rushed to her aid, not realizing what on earth could be the matter, for — horror of horrors — *nothing was visible*. It is perhaps just this *invisibility* that is so terrifying. Because what then is causing the agony of the victim?

The woman was in the throes of massive muscle spasms. Her body jerked, she gasped for air, emitting screams which soon turned into a frothy gurgling. Then all at once, silence. A silence that

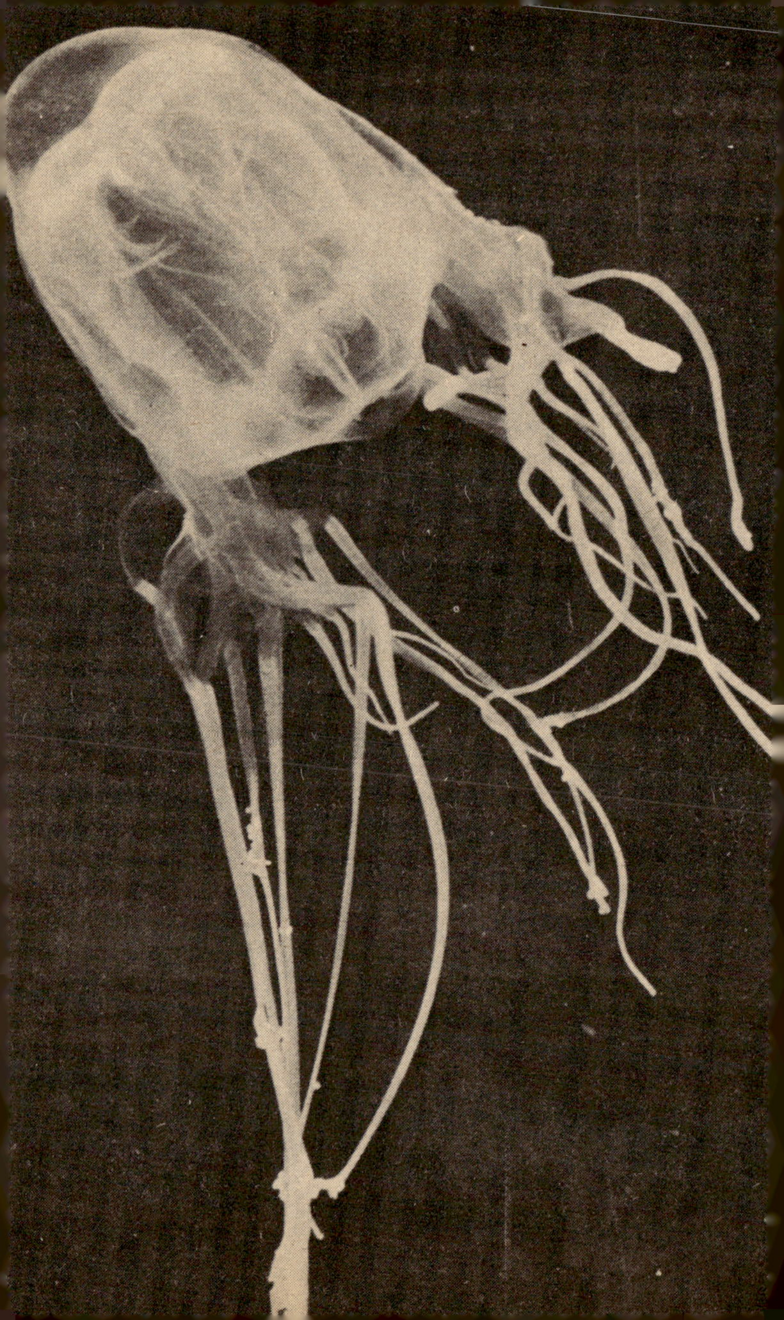

was worse to the horrified onlookers than her screaming. It was all over. Two or three minutes had passed. And she was dead. Her heart had stopped — paralyzed.

"No agony can be greater than this," the doctor said grimly. As quickly as he had come, he was still too late.

And, as someone observed, "What good could he have done anyway?"

Perhaps by now a reliable vaccine and antivenin exists. Let us hope so; maybe then those ninety-odd victims of this deadliest of marine animals — this creature from the blackest, most ghoulish nightmares — will not have died in vain.

THE GREATEST PREDATOR

While it has long been the great whale or the giant octopus who has commanded the lurid imagination of horror writers, and of mankind in general, today it is the shark who has finally reached top billing. This is not to say that the shark was not always up there near the top; only that with the popularity of the recent books and films, the great white shark has been able to thrill and terrorize the imaginations of millions of people.

Why this massive fear of sharks? No doubt it is not too distantly allied to the basic fear of being eaten alive. The shark — let's face it — does eat people alive. He can and he will and he *does*.

Through the centuries sharks have proven to be marvelously adaptable. As a matter of fact, biologically sharks are quite primitive. At the same time they are among the world's most dangerous and efficient predators. They are all but invincible.

Mobility of a high order is common to the shark. He and his relative, the ray, are different from the other higher fishes in that their skeleton consists of cartilage and not one true bone. Cartilage is of course lighter than bone and so is more buoyant.

Sharks apparently first appeared at the time of the Devonian Period, almost 400 million years ago. This was at the time when fishes were the dominant forms of life on the earth.

Of course, no one really knows how the shark began; ancient shark remains usually consist of teeth or their spines only since cartilage does not last well. Relics of sharks have been found that date back about 300 million years. Some of these ancient beasts, pieced together by paleontologists, reveal that today's killer is not very different from its ancestor — only that the mouth then opened at the front of the snout, whereas today it is underslung.

Fossil shark teeth six inches long have been unearthed. From this the size of the owner can be imagined; comparing it to the teeth in a modern shark — a thirty six-foot great white shark whose jaws are in the British Museum of Natural History — with a tooth length of three inches, the ancient shark may have been twice as large.

As a rule, sharks are large, with the whale shark — the biggest — reaching sixty feet. The whale shark tips the scales at ten tons and is the largest living fish. On the other hand, the midwater shark, only six inches long, seems like a minnow in comparison.

Sharks live all over the globe. They cruise at 12,000 feet and they also skim along the surface of the water. They penetrate many of the great rivers for several hundred miles, they visit lakes and lagoons — freshwater has never been uncongenial to them.

Nearly all serious writers on the subject refer to the great white shark as a true monster of the sea. He is a true man-eater. Whenever this brute — *Carcharodon carcharias* — has addressed himself to human beings the experience has inevitably been harrowing. Death, destruction, terror and tragedy have been the fruits of his attention.

One of the most frightful encounters ever recorded was an attack on a fourteen-foot dory on July 9, 1953, of Cape Breton Island, **Nova Scotia.** A huge fish suddenly smashed into the dory, blasting an eight-inch hole in the bottom of the boat. The two male occupants were hurled into the water and one of them drowned. The shark was identified later — on the basis of a tooth imbedded in the boat's wooden hull — as a white shark about twelve feet long.

Any shark is a potential menace, no matter his size. They appear to attack humans when the person triggers the appropriate patterns of feeding behavior in the fish. For instance, it is wise not to thrash around when you are in water which might have sharks nearby; and it is definitely unwise to trail a string of speared fish while skin diving.

It may safely be stated that shark attacks can **take place wherever men and sharks share the** water. While shark incidents seem more common in the tropics, they are not unpopular in colder climes. As a rule, most attacks take place within a fairly broad area, between latitudes thirty degrees north and thirty degrees south. It appears that South Africa and Australia suffer the greatest problem with shark attack.

Consider that these beasts have voracious appetites. A regular staple of their diet is the man-sized animal. Sharks have been known to chew hooks that have been baited with their own entrails after they have been gutted and thrown back into the sea.

One of the most terrifying situations is the feeding frenzy. While many shark attacks involve only one animal, when there is a source of food at hand large numbers of sharks will often appear, thus starting a feeding frenzy that is without doubt one of the most bloodcurdling sights imaginable. Gangs of sharks literally tear their victims to shreds, savaging huge chunks of flesh from the prey as well as from each other in their berserk quest for food. The beasts, ravenous to the point of mania, churn the water to a bloody froth, leaping high into the air, and attacking each other.

When a ship goes down or when a plane falls into the sea with many people aboard there is great danger that a feeding frenzy will occur.

And yet, even while there was no feeding frenzy, a horrific occurrence took place when there was a shipwreck in the Caribbean Sea one November day in 1819.

Apparently the ship *Una* ran onto a rock about sixty miles offshore, smashed its bow and therefore made it necessary for the crew and sixty five black laborers on board to abandon ship.

The crew swiftly took to the boats while the

poor blacks climbed onto pieces of wreckage that floated on the water.

The sea was calm, so it has been reported. But presently its smooth surface was broken by the fins of sharks — some, it is said, from eight to sixteen feet in length. Some of the men fell off the wreckage and into the jaws of the sharks. Now, emboldened, with their appetites whetted, the sharks began to attack the larger pieces of wreckage to which the men were clinging. In a short while the men were screaming in terror as the sharks beat at them with their snouts right out of the water, rammed the spars and timbers and hatches, and submarined them. One by one the men were eaten by the sharks. There were no survivors.

A shark swims with a thrust, a sideways sweep of its tail fin, and it is powerful. It is estimated that the mako shark probably reaches a speed of twenty two knots.

While it is the shark's teeth that is of most concern to humans, his skin does cause lacerations on humans. This is not surprising since it is covered not with scales, like so many fishes, but with decticles, structures which biologically are similar to teeth.

Of course, the shark's actual teeth are fantastic. These, in most species, are sharp as the proverbial razor. Moreover, they are set in jays which can mount a pressure of several tons per square inch, with the consequence that it's a simple matter to shear bone and flesh.

The shape of a shark's tooth is the result of its diet. Those that eat **mollusks** have teeth with flat surfaces in order to crush and grind shells. Sharks than dine on lobsters and moderate-sized fish have teeth that are like spikes so that they can spear and hold their prey. And those sharks which hunt large fish such as tuna and seals have teeth like blades, with serrated edges that shear off enormous chunks of flesh.

But whatever the size or shape of those great fangs, the *supply* of teeth is inexhaustible. A shark's teeth have no sockets and so they fall out fairly easily. This is of small moment, however, because they are replaced almost instantly. In the jaws behind the first row of teeth are row upon row of others still growing and developing and ready to step into the front ranks.

There is no question that it is the great white shark that has received the "lion's share" of the publicity in regard to attacks upon humans. But his relatives are not much less rapacious and effective. It would be wise simply to regard all sharks as dangerous.

In the U.S. Navy publication *Science in the Sea*, J. W. Lermond maintains that between 50 and 65 percent of the victims of shark attack die. If the victim is not eaten alive he usually expires from shock and loss of blood. But the question arises: What is the complex group of factors that triggers shark attack? There are certain evident patterns. For instance, frequency of attack seems to favor waters that are warmer than sixty-five degrees Fahrenheit, but possibly this is merely an indication that people don't like to swim so much in cold water or that the more dangerous sharks like warm water.

At the same time, evidence from a study that has been reported in the journal *Science* reveals that staying close to shore is no protection against the attack of a shark. Survey shows that of 217 shark attacks where the distance from shore was known, more than half of these occurred within 200 feet of the beach. In other cases where the distance from shore was not always known, 75 out of 302 victims of attack were standing in water no deeper than their shoulders, and 212 persons were hit by sharks in water that was no deeper than five feet.

Perhaps the first thing to realize is that a person becomes a potential victim of a shark when he provokes one or when he somehow triggers certain mechanisms that make the shark go after prey. For instance, the shart automatically responds to certain stimuli such as the thrashing about of a fish that has been wounded, or one that is sick. The shark, like other animals, goes for prey that is the easiest to catch, such as an injured or sick fish. And so, if a human being thrashes about in that same manner he may trigger the same response.

Sharks also appear able to pick up sound vibrations at six hundred yards. Because the vibrations of a struggling fish travel through the water, they are easily sensed by a shark. Sharks also have an uncanny sense of smell. It is said that a shark can sense the slightest trace of blood in millions of gallons of water.

And so, certain actions by humans in the water will increase the possibility of shark attack. For instance, if one acts like an injured fish, one is inviting sharks. Erratic swimming can send out vibrations. Juices from a speared fish, or even contrastic colors of a diver's suit or air tank can attract the shark's attention.

Shark repellents do not seem to be the surest thing. Researchers working with the Navy have developed a man-size plastic bag that floats in the water by means of an inflatable collar. It is called the Shark screen. It's five feet long and three feet wide when inflated, but it folds easily into a small package that can be carried on a life jacket.

Edward R. Ricciuti, in his fine book *Killers of the Seas,* says that probably the best antishark weapon so far is the Navy's "Shark Dart" which frogmen have carried since 1971 for the Apollo spacecraft splashdowns.

The Shark Dart is a hollow steel dart that carries a highly compressed carbon dioxide cartridge. It is usually mounted on the end of a lance or spear; and when it is driven into the body of the shark, the cartridge explodes and releases carbon dioxide into the shark's body cavity. The gas sends the shark to the surface, rather like a balloon, and he floats helplessly with his insides ruptured.

The protection of swimmers from sharks is still one of the most important problems at beaches where attacks from the underwater menace are common.

Thus far the best method seems to be meshing, a method whereby gill nets are placed in a staggered pattern beyond the breaker line. The idea is to trap the sharks rather than simply to prevent them from reaching closer to shore.

Basically, swimmers, divers and other possible victims of disasters at sea can lessen the threat of shark attack by remembering the adaptations that have made the shark so effective over the centuries. Since the sharks eyes are adapted for seeing contrast it is foolish for a person to wear a black-and-white swimming costume or shiny jewelry in water inhabited by sharks. And because the shark can so easily pick up vibrations caused by movement in the water, it is not wise to make erratic movements. And finally, if you have cut yourself and are bleeding, get out of the water pronto. And never carry a line of fish that you have speared. The temptation to a shark would simply be too great.

H. David Baldridge mentions the same "suit" problem in his book *Shark Attack*. He says that divers should be careful not to dress in attire that may resemble an animal such as the seal upon which the shark is inclined to dine. He concludes that this might have been the big factor in a fatal attack on a skin diver a few years ago in the waters of Western Australia.

Robert Bartle, age twenty-three, and a friend were spearfishing in water about twenty-five feet deep that was fairly murky. They were about eight hundred yards off Jurien Bay which is 130 miles north of Perth. The date was August 19, 1967. Bartle was clad in a black wetsuit with bright yellow seams, a black headcover and black flippers. His legs were bare for the pants were short. His friend was wearing a full black wetsuit.

They had not yet speared any fish. Bartle dove at

one point to recover a dropped float line, while his friend swam ahead, out toward the open sea.

In the words of his companion: "The shark came the opposite way and went straight under me about eight feet down. It came out of the blue like a rocket and grabbed him (Bartle). It moved so fast that by the time I looked back it had Bob in its mouth and was shaking Bob like a leaf. I rolled over immediately, dived and placed a spear in its head. It broke Bob in half and rose up at me with Bob's legs and flippers sticking out of its mouth. Bob's upper half floated to the surface. The shark began circling slowly. It made one pass at me, and I poked my speargun in the direction of its eye. The gun struck behind its right eye, and a membrane appeared to cover its eye in a lateral plane.

"Realizing I was helpless, I retrieved Bob's gun which was floating near his body. As the shark passed by once more, I endeavored to spear it in the eye. However, the spear passed over the shark. In his circling motion, he tangled this spear around Bob's float line and my spear line.

"I moved from the pool of blood and watched for some movements. The shark did not appear to be feeding. Bob's feet and flippers were still projecting from its mouth. The jaw must have been two and a half feet wide. As there was nothing further that could be done, I swam towards shore . . . "I returned approximately 90 to 100 minutes later (with three crayfishermen), and the shark had moved approximately 150 to 200 yards south.

"The spear was still embedded and tangled around Bob's float. We pulled my gun aboard, cut the cord and made it fast to a stanchion; the idea of this was to reload and spear the shark again. Unfortunately the shark managed to break free before we were ready. The shark was not seen again. The upper portion of his (Bartle's) body was not mutilated in any way after the attack."

Theories followed, the chief of which appeared to be that this attack and others which involved skin divers in South Australian waters could have been due to the divers in their black wetsuits and flippers being mistaken for seals upon which the great white sharks in that area were known to feed. In each case, apparently, the victim had been suddenly attacked, with no warning, but had not been completely eaten.

Rodney Fox was more fortunate. He lived to tell the tale of his horrifying adventure with the great white shark.

On the morning of August 12, 1963, Fox, aged twenty three, had been competing with about forty other divers in the South Australian spearfishing championships at Alding Reef, which is about thirty five miles south of Adelaide.

A lot of fish had been speared, and blood covered a wide area on the outgoing tide. This must have formed a track over which the shark traveled in search of prey.

Fox had been ashore weighing his morning catch and was now beginning to go after another fish, close to the drop-off to a forty-foot depth some three quarters of a mile from shore.

He was wearing a full black wetsuit with yellow stripes down each side of the body, arms, and legs.

Fox has told how he was moving slowly toward his target with his speargun poised to fire when all of a sudden he found himself pushed through the water with his chest in the jaws of a shark. His gun had been knocked out of his hand.

"There was no pain, although I felt quite weak. My mind was very clear, and all I could think of was 'you'd better get out of here.' My left hand was on top of the shark, and my right hand was free.

"I tried to gouge his eyes with my fingers, pushing them in any cavity in its head, when he let go of me."

Fox went on to say that he wasn't sure whether or not he had managed to gouge the shark's eyes.

"Instinctively, I pushed at the shark and I felt my hand gash on its teeth and I retracted my hand quickly, cutting it deeply again on the way out. Both my knees were against the shark's side, so I **put both my arms and legs around it, thinking that it couldn't bite me in this position.**"

Rodney Fox realized that he would need air sooner or later so he let go and headed quickly for the surface. When he reached the surface and had taken in air he saw the shark coming for him again. The water was very red with blood and his face mask was half off.

"The next few moments were the most terrifying for me as I thought that 'if he has another go at me, I'm finished.' I pushed at him with my foot, and I felt my flipper touch him. Next thing, the fish buoy which I had been towing on thirty feet of cord disappeared, the cord went tight, and I was dragged under water again. I was trying to find the quick release catch on my belt when the cord broke, and I came to the surface.

"The patrol boat saw that I was in trouble before I yelled, 'SHARK!' because of the blood in the water and my face mask being missing. They came and dragged me out of the water and, at that time, I gave up fighting for myself and lay semiconscious in the boat, relying on them to do their best for me.

"Blood was pouring out of the gashes in my suit, and they could see into the large gash in my side, which, every time I breathed, sucked in air. Bunching me up — to keep the wounds together — I was taken ashore, place on a board stretcher and into a car which sped toward Adelaide and hospital.

"Nine miles down the road the ambulance, which had been rung for me, met the car and I was transferred into it, given oxygen, and raced to hospital.

"My biggest problem was breathing. I remember that it was perhaps the hardest thing I have ever done in my life. I would have given up many times but two friends of mine who were with me all the way to hospital kept talking to me, and telling me to keep fighting and that I was going to be all right."

Thus the account of an extraordinary brave man. Rodney Fox did recover. He carries beneath his left armpit a stark reminder of his close brush with death in the form of large semicircles of tooth marks of the great white shark, front and back, **reaching from his shoulder and upper arm almost to**

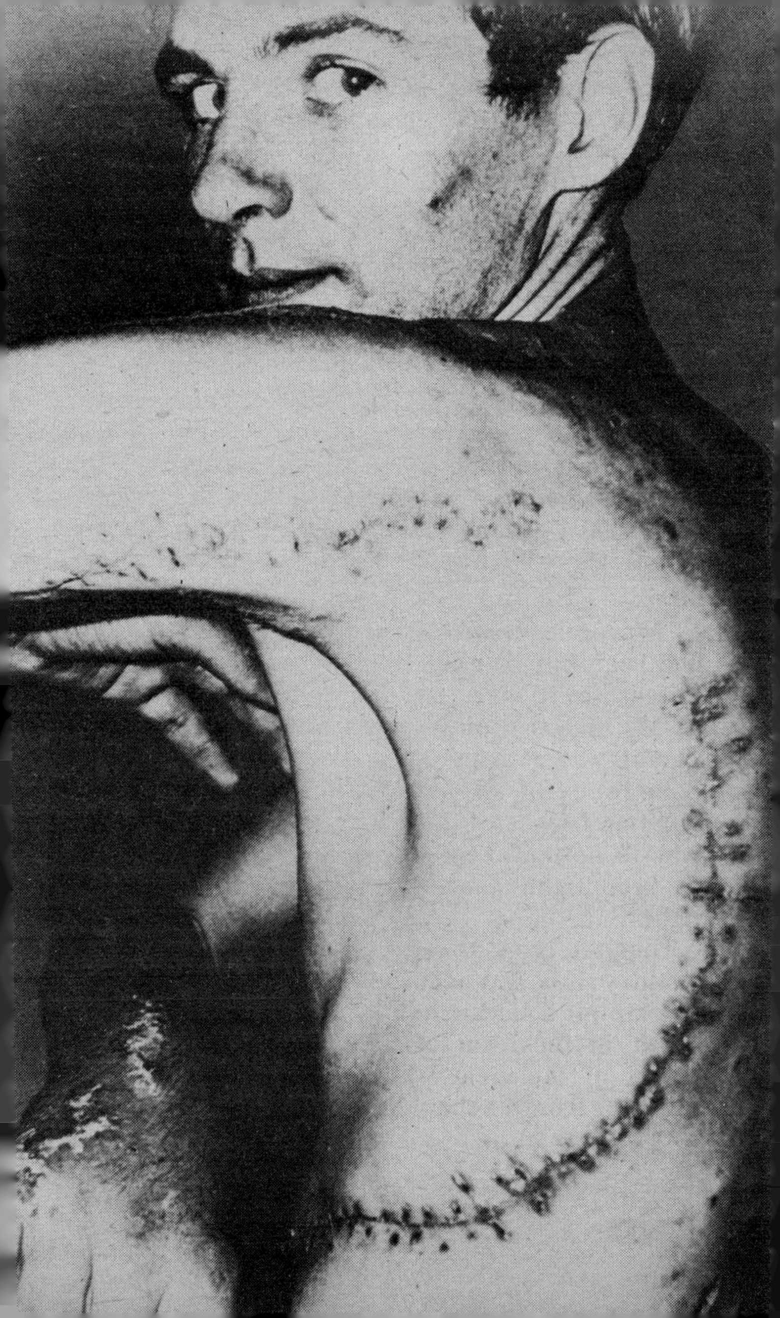

his waist.

To live to tell the tale!

Australian skin diver Henri Bource had a narrow escape. On November 29, 1964 Bource and a group of skin and scuba divers were photographing and even playing with a group of seals in thirty feet of water about 100 yards off Lady Julia Percy Island, Australia. Bource and two friends in wetsuits were playing with a bull seal about 60 yards or so from the boat and about 100 yards from shore when one member of the diving party who was on the beach saw a great dorsal fin slicing the water and going right for the divers.

It went right past a group of females and seal calves that were playing on a reef, went on through the center of the group of seals near the divers and disappeared into the water just about twenty feet from the men.

Maybe a minute later people watching on the beach saw Bource rise bodily out of the water as the shark hit him.

Later, Bource said: "We were free diving. . . to maintain close contact with the seals and note their reactions to the divers. We singled out a large bull seal and commenced to play with it. It did not indicate any objections but seemed to enjoy the company of the divers. At one stage the seal dived to the bottom, and as I turned to meet its return to the surface I felt a severe grab at my left leg. . . . I knew immediately by the severeness of the grip that this could only be a shark.

"The impact carried me free of the surface, at which time I yelled, 'SHARK' several times. I was then pulled underwater...both my mask and snorkel had been lost on impact. I was pulled down approximately twenty feet and all the time felt the characteristic shaking of the shark's head.... I was able to feel the shark's head with my left arm and distinctly remember trying to locate the eyes as a possible vulnerable spot; with my right foot, I tried to kick at the shark's mouth...I estimate my time of submersion as approximately three quarters of a minute before I felt my leg being torn off.... If it hadn't come off I would have drowned. I was then able to surface and found myself surrounded by blood."

The two divers who were close to Bource came instantly to his assistance and used their hand-held spears to prevent the shark from biting again. The brute made several close passes through the bloody water as it followed the three men toward the swiftly approaching boat.

With the help of the other divers Bource was taken aboard the boat and a tourniquet was put on his left leg which had been cleanly severed at the knee.

Bource's life was saved because of the speedy first aid and the foresight to radio ahead for blood of the correct type and medical assistance to be waiting on their arrival on the beach.

The shark was twelve to fourteen feet in length, and identified either as a tiger shark or great white shark; the evidence leaned toward the latter.

It has been recorded that one of the divers who had been alongside Bource felt the body of the shark bump against his leg, evidently as the great beast was still tearing at Bource. Then he saw the shark heading down to the bottom with blood streaming from its mouth and a flipper hanging from its clenched jaws.

It is not usual that a shark is captured and absolutely identified as being the one responsible for a particular strike. But on February 26, 1966 a great white shark, measuring eight feet three inches was not only captured but brought to shore still attached to the leg of its victim, a thirteen-year-old boy named Raymond Short.

Young Short was bathing, along with about fifty other people, at Coledale Beach on the South Coast of New South Wales, Australia.

The beach was shallow, actually a sandy cover with a bottom that slid easily out to the sea. It was a lovely day, for this time of year is Australian summer, since that continent is below the Equator.

The water was slightly murky for there had been some heavy sea the previous week. Short had just started to tread water when he was gripped first on the left thigh and then on the lower part of the right leg.

He related: "I remember treading water when I felt something nudge my right leg. I kicked my leg, but it felt like it had something heavy attached to it."

The boy was dragged under the water a number of times, and then at last realized that a shark was holding him. He kicked it several times, but the beast would not let go.

"Then I began punching, but it was still lying there as if it were dead. I tried to swim back to the beach but still could not get rid of it. I was beginning to panic when I thought that if I bit it, it just might go away. I remember doubling over and biting it hard on the nose."

Young Short cried for help, but the other bathers fled from the water as the shark warning bell was rung. Then Short said to the lifeguard who reached him, "Help me, please — the shark is still there."

The lifeguard could not see the shark in the murky water and only realized it was really there when, at Short's insistence, he ran his hand down the boy's leg and felt it.

By then, other lifeguards had appeared, and when one of them moved the youngster's leg the shark was exposed for the first time.

Another man instantly clubbed the brute with a surfboard, but it still held its grip. At that point, as gently as possible, the men half carried, half dragged both the shark and the boy to the beach. Here the shark's jaws were forced open and at last the boy was released.

Fortunately, a hospital was nearby and Short arrived there less than ten minutes after the time of the attack. He was in deep shock and had lost a severe amount of blood. The calf muscles and all muscular tissue on the posterior part of the right leg were lost. The shinbone was cleanly exposed and it bore imprints of the shark's teeth along its entire length. Multiple lacerations were on the front and back of the left thigh, and both the boy's hands were badly cut. But Raymond Short re-**covered, and with the assistance of a brace, he began to regain the use of his withered right leg.**

The shark which had bitten into Short's leg died on the beach. It was definitely an eight-foot three-inch female great white shark. Examination showed that the shark had suffered tremendous wounds of recent origin, one wound being clearly the bite of another shark. It has been suggested that the wounds were probably the reason for the shark's strange lack of aggression while Short was being rescued. And so Raymond Short was lucky indeed — thanks to another shark, to the swift action of the men on the beach, and to his own courage.

What appears again and again in our research — really like a refrain — is the note of heroism, both on the part of the victims and on the part of those who come to their aid. It's no joke to plunge into the water and battle with a wild blood-berserk shark who is in the act of savaging a human being into pieces; yet, again and again, rescuers and would-be rescuers have risked their own lives and limbs to help a fellow human being.

THE BRAVE ACTRESS

It was an early afternoon in late January, 1963, and the sun was hot along the beach at Sugarloaf Bay. It was summer, a time for holiday makers in Australia. Middle Harbor, Sydney was an ideal spot to go digging for oysters.

The popular young actress Marcia Hathaway thought so. And so did her fiance, Frederick Knight, a thirty-eight-year-old journalist. The couple were on a picnic trip with five friends in a small cruiser. That day they had decided to drop anchor in Sugarloaf Bay and go looking for their supper.

Miss Hathaway was well known among her friends and in the theater as a brilliant and versatile actress and a "deeply religious person." Her career was highly successful, and she was still young. Her success extended to the stage, to radio and television. Apparently all who met her were impressed by her gentle demeanor and her intelligence.

That afternoon at Sugarloaf Bay the water was

calm. The oyster pickers worked at knee depth, twenty yards from shore.

No one saw the shark. No one heard him. Everyone was happy; they were having a marvelous time. Marcia Hathaway and Frederick Knight were especially joyous for they were to announce their engagement formally on her birthday on February 8, less than two weeks away.

The shark slid silently through the calm, murky, and shallow water. There wasn't even a ripple to announce his presence.

Suddenly — as Knight related later — "I heard Marcia scream and turning to her I saw her being dragged into deeper water. I raced to her, caught her arms and began a tug-of-war with whatever it was holding her."

Marcia Hathaway thought at first she was caught by an octopus. But now Knight saw that it was a shark.

One of their friends, who was on the beach and had his back to the couple, reported: "I heard a scream, looked round and thought they were just skylarking. I continued looking for oysters. Then I heard a second scream and this time when I turned I saw the water was bloodstained and foaming."

James Delmege heroically raced into the water to help Knight get his fiancee away from the shark.

Knight meanwhile had straddled the shark. At one point he related that he felt his foot in its mouth. "If felt soft and spongy." He punched the shark, and kicked it. But to no purpose. The water was whipped into a red foam as the men battled the monster.

The two heroic men finally won their tug-of-war, but at a fearful cost. The shark had caught the girl below the calf on the right leg, then in a second lunge had embedded his sabre-sharp teeth into her upper right thigh near the hip.

When the two men carried the poor girl to the beach they saw that her right leg was torn almost completely off. All three were covered in blood and close to severe shock.

By now the other members of the party aboard the cruiser had seen the attack and had rowed quickly ashore in the dinghy with sheets they had pulled from the cabin bunks.

On the beach they applied tourniquets. But the poor girl's leg was too badly mauled for this to be of much use. Now they lifted her and placed her carefully in the boat and rowed back to the cruiser.

All this took time, with the poor girl bleeding heavily. As soon as they were all aboard they took the cruiser to a nearby boat shed where Knight dove overboard and swam about twenty yards to a house to get the occupants to telephone for an ambulance.

He swam back to the cruiser and they made for Mowbray Point where they were met by an ambulance.

But now occurred one of those horrendous mishaps of the sort that seem to come only from the wildest fiction.

By now Miss Hathaway was unconscious; and the ambulance attendants having loaded her into the ambulance, used oxygen in an attempt to revive her. But because of the steep grade leading up from

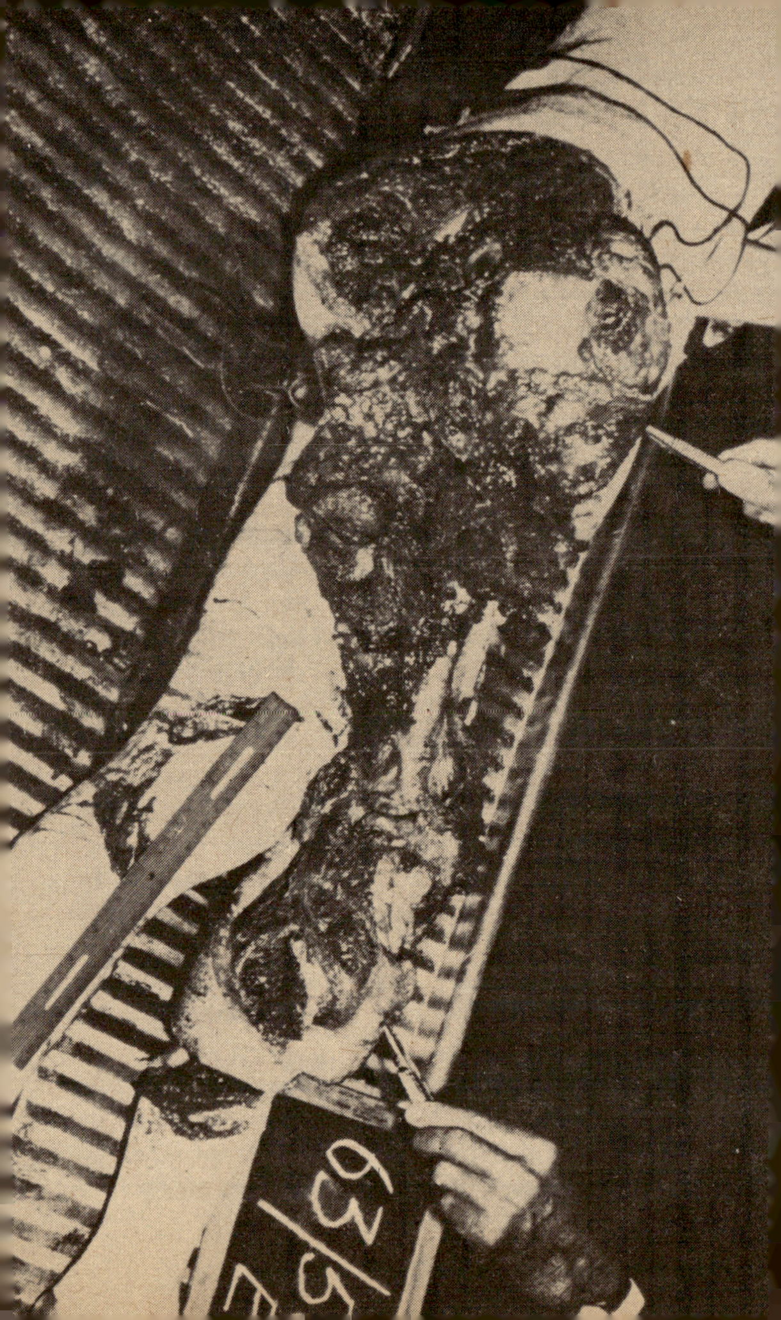

the water's edge and the slippery surface, the ambulance clutch burned out. Although some thirty people tried desperately to push the vehicle, the grade was too steep. A reporter who had reached the scene now radioed his office and a second ambulance was dispatched.

But to no avail. The poor girl had no chance. She had suffered a gaping wound on the anterior part of the right thigh with severance of the femoral artery, another gaping wound on the buttock, and other lacerations on the right calf, left thigh and left hand. Her right leg was as good as off at the hip.

And yet, with marvelous courage, she rallied for a few moments. And when her fiance asked her if she hurt very much, she said, "No, I am not in pain," and then she added: "Don't worry about me, dear. God will look after me."

These were her last words.

Tooth fragments taken from her leg showed that she had been killed by a whale shark. And a day or two later a bronze whale shark, ten feet in length, was caught about 100 yards from the place of the attack. It was thought that this was the killer.

THE GREATEST MONSTER

Who is the deadliest, the most horrifying monster of them all? Who is it that strikes unparalleled terror into the hearts of old and young, rich and poor? Who but that massive, multiarmed beast with those bulbous eyes and slimy grip, whose suction cups and suffocating embrace have brought so many divers, swimmers — yes, and even ships filled with men — to the bottom of the sea. Perhaps *his* sea.

With the present exception of the great white shark — courtesy of *Jaws* and other literary and cinematic efforts — and, in former times, the great whale, it is the octopus without question who has received the brisk and horrified attention of writers, movie makers, tellers of horror tales to children and adults, and whoever it is who makes up those terrifying dreams.

The giant octopus is without doubt the most awesome, the most feared, the greatest sea monster ever to slice through the great silent waters of the

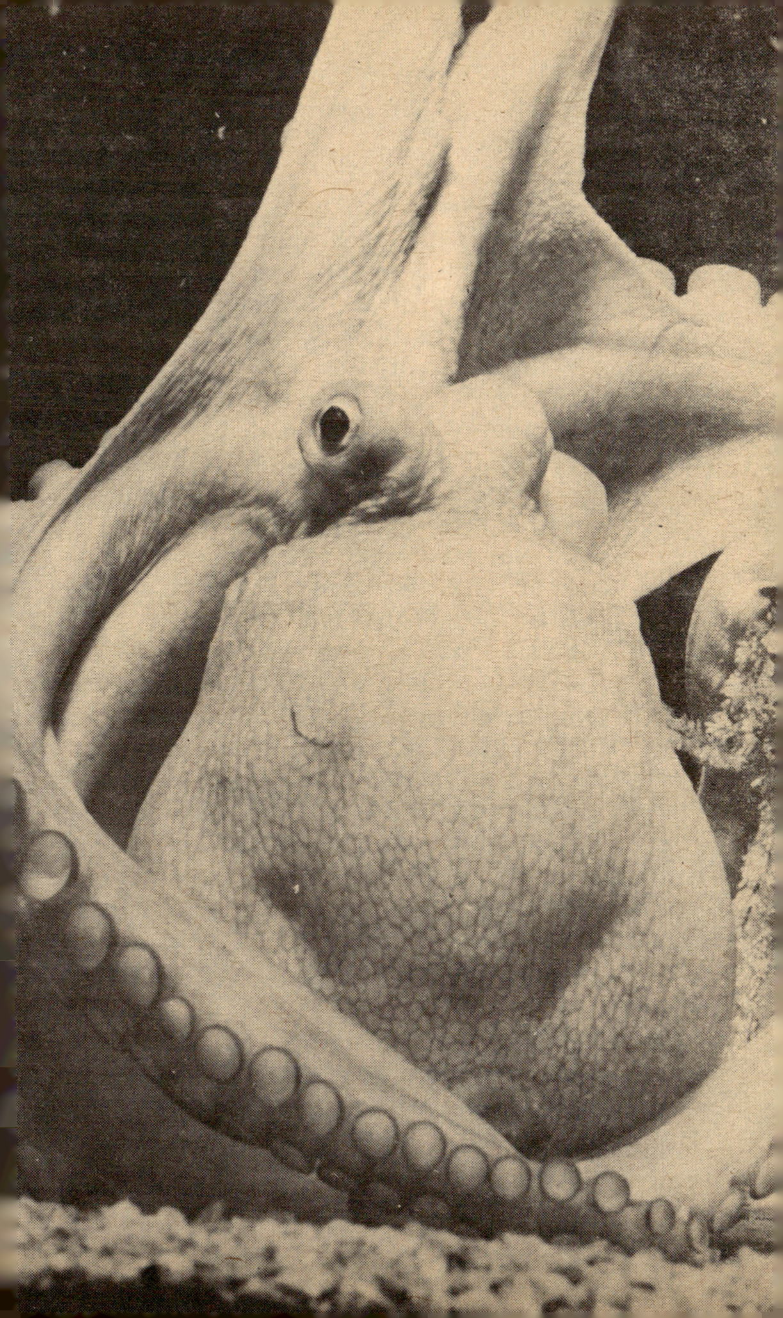

deep, striking terror over the centuries into the hearts and bowels of countless thousands of readers and viewers.

At the mere thought of the giant octopus one's blood runs cold. His hideous aspect, his *slither and slide,* the horror of his touch upon one's cringing, ice-cold body is enough to kill a man right there.

And yet most surprising — and therefore in our view, much more terrifying — is the fact that it isn't really the great monster octopus who is so lethal. Far more dangerous, much more deadly — though hardly known by anyone at all — is a quite tiny member of the octopus family. A charming, beautifully iridescent little creature with an arm spread of a mere three to four inches.

Fearsome? But who could ever fear such a tiny thing, such an attractive member of the marine world with his beautiful colors! Why, you might certainly wish to pick him up and play with him, since he really does have all the luster of a charming peacock. And people have indeed picked up *Hapalochlaena maculosa* and played with him.

For, after all, we have learned from our books that, actually, most little octopuses are harmless. They are frequently curious, but shy, and they tend to hide in holes and caves. Lots of people, even schoolchildren, have picked up one of these adorable little creatures and brought it home as a pet. As a rule, they have not lived very long to tell about it.

On June 22, 1967 James Albert Ward, age twenty-three, a private in the Australian army, was exploring some rock pools in the Camp Cover area near Sydney. With him were two other soldier friends, Private Michael Novak, age eighteen, and Private Stephen Arthurson, also eighteen.

These young men had in fact only joined the army the day before and were stationed at nearby Watson's Bay.

It was Private Novak who gave evidence at the City Coroner's Court, along with the curator of the marine biology department of the Australian Museum.

"There was just the three of us," Novak told the court, "We were walking at Camp Cove. We had a couple of hours off."

Novak was described as a blond young man with a frank expression, blue eyes, about an inch under six feet. Frightened. Very frightened by the dreadful experience he had shared.

"It could just as easily have been me or Stephen," he told reporters.

"We were just walking along and Jim called to me. I looked where he was pointing. He was standing right at the edge of a rock pool and when I looked I saw something very bright blue. Then we saw it was a very small octopus. Only about four or five inches across. A beautiful little thing."

This was verified by measurements taken by medical authorities. The actual octopus measured three and a half inches in arm spread.

Novak said, "Jim reached down and sort of put his finger toward the octopus, sort of like he was playing, like you would with a kitten. And Stephen came over and we watched the little thing curl around Jim's hand. And Jim picked him up."

Michael Novak paused in his testimony then. He was clearly having trouble going on.

He took a deep breath and then continued. "Well, it was time to get back to barracks, and so Jim picked him up and off we went." He paused and added, "I noticed then that the octopus was a bright bluish purple and sometimes he would turn pink."

It was about twenty minutes after he had picked up the tiny octopus that Private Ward began to have difficulty breathing, and he complained of feeling dizzy.

"See if you can get him off my hand," he said to his two friends. "I can't get him off. I think he has poisoned me!"

And suddenly he began shaking his hand while his voice broke in a scream. "Get it off me! Get it off me!"

But Novak was unable to get the little beast to release itself from Jim Ward's hand. He pulled and pulled. Stephen Arthurson then came to help and together they managed to wrench the deadly little beast from its victim.

"My God, it's poisoned me!" screamed Ward. "Get me to a doctor, get me to a doctor!" And he started into a run, but stopped suddenly, his chest heaving, his face turning purple. And he began to retch and vomit. In a moment he fell to his knees, his hand clutching at his heart, his eyes starting out of his head, his face almost black and twisted in terror and pain.

The two young men helped him the rest of the way to the barracks where a sergeant drove them instantly to the medical center.

Five doctors worked on Ward to keep him alive as arrangements were made to transport him to Prince Henry Hospital where an iron lung and a team of doctors were waiting.

The doctors now gave Ward oxygen, mouth-to-mouth resuscitation, and applied external heart massage in the medical center and again in the ambulance as they sped to the hospital.

There, they continued the treatment while Ward lay writhing on the operating table.

The doctors worked swiftly, with marvelous control. They knew what they — and Ward — were up against.

Actually, the bite of this tiny octopus is painless, or nearly so, but this makes it all the more dangerous for there is no warning.

Victims who have recovered from that bite tell that they have experienced a numbness in the mouth and head, difficulty in breathing, vomiting, erractic muscular control, paralysis of the chest, and complete paralysis — in that sequence.

According to a 1968 publication of the Commonwealth Serum Laboratories, "Pharmacologically the venom, which is derived from large salivary glands, affects both nerve conductivity and neuro-muscular junctions. Complete and rapid cessation of all voluntary muscle activity, including that of the diaphragm, is induced. If death occurs it is due to respiratory failure." *Hapalochlaena maculosa* is common in certain Australian waters, and is found in crevices, rock pools and in underwater caves down to a depth of between twenty-five and thirty feet.

At the Third Australian Medical Congress in Sydney, Dr. J. Trinka, Deputy Director of the Commonwealth Serum Laboratories, said, "Australian snakes are considered the deadliest in the world but they are no comparison to the blue-ringed octopus."

Indeed, just a trace of this creature's venom in the water with a crab will convulse the crustacean and paralyze it. What the venom does to a human is to in effect destroy the functioning of the neuromuscular system. It blocks, in a word, the conduction of nerve impulses, and so halts the body's voluntary muscular action and prevents the victim from breathing.

Now, as the doctors worked with every ounce of their ability on the writhing Ward, he began to vomit. Now it looked as though he was trying to gather himself for a gigantic scream of pain, and maybe rage. But the poor man was not able. For he was paralyzed, trapped in an armored agony from which there was only one escape. It came just ninety minutes after he had been bitten by the little blue-ringed octopus.

The only marks that could be found on his body were two tiny bruises on the second knuckle of his left hand.

THE VAMPIRES

I had just started to see San Payana's mountain when I heard it.

"It's a hell of a time for the damn engine to miss," Joe, my radio operator, said.

I didn't answer him, I just kept listening to the splutter as the small plane started to wobble. I'd been flying the mail on the Peru-Paraguay-Chile route for three years and I was already looking for a likely place to land if the engine really went out.

Suddenly it caught, lost it, then caught and held. I breathed a real sigh at that.

"Where are we?" I asked Joe.

"About ten minutes now." He coughed. "All clear for San Filippe."

I was feeling tired now. But I thought of the break at San Filippe where I'd get a meal and lots of coffee that would keep me going for the rest of the route that night.

"And we'll have the ground crew double check," I told Joe. "Send it over the wire."

We landed without any more engine trouble. I knew we were both relieved. As a rule the stop was only fifteen minutes, while we picked up and dropped mail and an occasional passenger. But the check out took a good twenty minutes more. I'd try to make up some of it in the air.

"All checked out," Joe said as he climbed in.

"Who's the passenger?" I asked.

"Newspaper. He's heading for Gran Carlina to do some kind of story."

I nodded toward the burly, middle-aged man who was seated behind us.

We rose abruptly and I glanced back at San Filippe. A cluster of lights, just breaking faintly into the gentle evening. A few stars, but faint. Night was coming and now I turned on my dial lights. Down below I saw lights in the villages.

The luminous dial hands were beginning to show up. All was going as it was meant to. The engine's 500 horsepower was like a well-broken steed — gentle, strong, responsive to my touch.

It must have been an hour out of San Filippe — in fact, when I checked I saw that it was just an hour — I felt as though someone was tugging at my shoulders. Yes — sudden heavy clouds smearing out the stars. I looked down, searching for village lights below.

Now the first tip of the storm touched us. Then it was as though it drew back — but only to suddenly smash at our craft. It was like a giant blow, and the little plane shuddered in every bolt and rivet.

Now the storm was all around us.

"How's the passenger?" I asked Joe.

"He just threw up, but he'll live. He hasn't got anywhere to go," he added with sardonic humor.

Now I gave up all idea of circumventing the storm. I could see it was too widespread for that. The lightning flashes led far inland. So I thought of trying to pass below it.

"We'll try under it."

I read my altitude as 5,500 feet and pressed the controls to bring the ship down. The engine started thudding violently and I was damn glad we'd had that checkup back at San Filippe. The plane quivered.

I corrected the gliding angle approximately and had Joe check his map for the height of the hills — some 1,600 feet. Just to be safe I determined to fly a touch above 2,000. It was sure risky. But I was always a gambler. And that storm didn't allow for much time in planning something.

A sudden eddy dragged us down, making the plane tremble still more harshly.

"It's probably local," I said. And I hoped I knew what I was talking about.

"If you say it," Joe answered, dubiously. I could tell he wasn't feeling too good about the way things were going.

Joe said, "Gran Carlina is signaling a sky only three-quarters overcast."

"Twenty minutes?"

"Right."

I looked back at our passenger. I thought he looked kind of greenish white, but I may have been putting that on him.

Several minutes passed, and the storm was really settling in.

"Where are we?" the passenger asked. I could hear the tremor behind his voice.

"Can't say exactly," I said. "Hell, we're flying by compass across a storm."

He didn't say anything to that.

I kept bending down every thirty seconds to check the gyroscope and compass. If there still remained a clear patch over Gran Carlina we would presently glimpse its lights across a cloud rift.

It was the promise of such a faint gleam that was leading me on. But just to make sure I scribbled a message to Joe.

"Don't know if I can get through. Ask if the weather's holding out behind."

The answer sent an appalling chill through me.

"Tanzanrey reports: Impossible return here. Storm."

"Get the San Fortanni weather report."

"San Fortanni reports west wind rising. Storm in the west. Sky three-quarters overcast. San Fortanni picking up badly on account of interferences. I'm having trouble too. I'll have to pull up the aerial on account of lightning. Are you going to turn back?"

"Shut up!" I told him. "Stop that damn chattering. Check on Cresta Banio."

"Cresta Banio reports: Violent westerly gale over Cresta Banio expected in less than fifteen minutes."

"Ask Gran Carlina."

"Gran Carlina reports: Westerly gale; a hundred

feet per second; rain squalls."

"Inform Asuncion: We are cut off on all sides; storm developing over a depth of seven hundred miles. No visibility. What shall we do?"

But the message Joe returned with was frightful. "Impossible communicate Asuncion. Can't even send. The shocks are too great."

I started to write a message, but the instant my hands left the controls to write, a great heave surged through my body and the whole plane rocked like a cork. I gave up.

And then I heard the crack. A wing? But we were going down. Plummeting. I couldn't see. The passenger was shouting.

And then we were below it. I was wrenching at the controls trying to pancake; there was no chance of avoiding a crash. But at last the night was clear. I couldn't see any lights. Where were we?

And there was water. A lake? We landed with a tremendous slap that almost tore me out of my seat.

"Oh my God," the newspaperman was saying. "Oh my God." Over and over. Joe was just swearing.

We had no idea where we were. Luckily we had landed at the edge of the lake, in shallow water, so there was no danger of the plane sinking. I could see we were in jungle country, pretty far off our course. Since it was still night we remained inside the plane, rather than risk a sortie into the unknown at the dead of night. The South American jungle is not the sort of place for an evening promenade.

We had light, fortunately, though we tried to conserve on it. The radio was smashed. No one was injured, save Joe who had a slight cut on his head, and myself with a mildly sprained ankle. The passenger, whose name was Francesco Conte, was in good spirits. I discovered why when we started passing around his bottle of Pisco.

Pisco is delightfully potent, and we warmed to it as a friend. It really got us through the night, keeping our courage up.

When dawn came we were hungry and pretty tired, but too tense really to think of sleep. Francesco was almost ebullient for he had addressed himself generously to the bottle.

"I can see the headlines," he told us, with a laugh. "Ace reporter crashes in jungle. Fights off horde of wild Indians. But heroically rescues crew of mail plane, etcetera, etcetera..."

"Sounds great," Joe said, sardonically.

The first thing we did was to rig up a signal consisting of a pole, which we hacked from a clump of bushes on the shore, and a shirt that made a sort of pennant.

"They'll be looking for us," Joe said.

I didn't want to remind him — or myself either, for that matter — how far off course we were.

"We can allay our hunger with some fish," Francesco said. "With the hatchet we can cut fishing poles and we must surely have some string or something in the plane."

"I *am* hungry," Joe said. "But are the fish okay? What kind of fish are there?"

"Piranhas," Francesco said, and he giggled. I

could see he'd had an ample share of the Pisco.

"But they are good to eat," he added. "I have been informed of that fact. The thing, of course, is to keep out of the way of those razor teeth."

We were looking at the water to see whether any fish were evident, but we saw nothing.

"Fortunately," Francesco said, with a big grin, holding up the empty bottle of Pisco, "fortunately, I had the presence of mind to bring another bottle. We are in good shape."

"Take it easy," I told him. "That's powerful stuff and we have empty stomachs. We'll need all our wits with us."

"Do not worry," Francesco said. "Soon we shall have delicious fish."

He had taken the hatchet and stepped to the shore and was chopping out a rod for fishing.

"What are we going to use for bait?" Joe asked. "We've got two candy bars left."

"Maybe the foil will attract them," I suggested. "Let's try it."

We could still see no fish, though the water was fairly clear. It was a bright day, and we were constantly scanning the sky for any sign of a plane.

"Are there natives, Indians?" Joe asked. "And how friendly are they?"

Nobody answered him. Francesco had his line baited — he had found twine and had rigged up a good fishing rod and had a bent pin for a hook — and he was sitting on the edge of the wing, with his legs crossed, fishing. He had taken another drink and was smiling.

Suddenly I saw his line bob. He felt it too and

pulled in when he felt the fish had really caught the hook.

"They are not piranhas," Francesco said.

"It looks like an eel of some kind," Joe said and he smashed it over the head. "Thank God they're not piranhas."

"We can use it for bait," I said. And then I noticed that the water around the wing of the plane was swarming with the little fish. They were not very large, but they were tremendously quick. There must have been hundreds of them.

All three of us were fishing by now, having fashioned poles, lines and hooks, and shortly we had a fair catch.

"We'll cook them on the bank," Francesco said. "Who knows what they are, but they could be quite tasty."

He was standing up, and had stripped off his clothes. "**I want to take a swim,**" he said, "I'm feeling cruddy and I want to dine in style."

"Maybe you shouldn't go in the water," I said. There was something about that horde of fish surging around our plane that somehow gave me a feeling of uneasiness.

"I'm just going to wade," Francesco said. He was standing on the wing and now he urinated into the water.

All at once the fish seemed to whip into a frenzy. They raced in such circles that the water really became alive. I didn't like it at all.

"That's the bait they like," Francesco said. "Pisco that has been refined and aged in the human body." He roared with boozy laughter. He took another drink. He was almost staggering now, for he had not eaten since before we left San Filippe and he had downed plenty of Pisco.

Suddenly, his foot slipped and he fell into the water. I only saw this out of the side of my eye, because at just that moment I thought I saw a plane.

"There's a plane!" I shouted.

At that very instant Francesco let out a scream and began clambering out of the water.

What happened then is hard to describe. I have never in my life seen anyone in such pain and terror as poor Francesco. He clambered onto the shore holding his groin, screaming at the top of his lungs.

Joe and I hurried to him. And then we saw what had happened. A fish had entered his penis. I grabbed at it, but missed.

"My God, get it out! Get it out!" He was screaming so loud his face had turned crimson. "Help me. God! Get it out! Help me!"

I grabbed the damn thing, but it was like trying to hold a wet saw. My hand slipped. It was covered with blood. The fish was worming its way up into Francesco's urethra. I could not get it out. It had sharp spines and had spread these to hold itself inside. I could see to my unbelievable horror that it was swelling — that is, the part that was still outside was swelling. A good three quarters of the creature was well inside the screaming Francesco.

I shall never forget it. We dragged him onto the plane and into the cabin, while he fought us, still screaming in the most frightful torment I have ever

Candiru (Cleveland Aquarium)

even imagined.

I could think of nothing else to do and so I hit him as hard as I could on the side of the jaw. I had been a boxer once and the punch was solid. He went out — mercifully. Knocked cold. Joe and I then tried to get the bloated creature out. Our hands were cut and bleeding, and finally we tried pliers. Nothing worked.

Francesco died right before our horrified eyes. Meanwhile, the revolting vampires swam wildly about the plane. I kicked those that we had caught back into the water and then vomited.

The plane had spotted us, and before nightfall a seaplane had come and landed on the lake. We were saved. Joe and I were saved. Poor, tragic Francesco certainly got his "story," his headline. He was the headline. It was a while before we found out from the men who picked us up that the fish that had entered his urethra was the candiru, otherwise known as the vampire catfish.

It was weeks later that Joe told me a chilling aspect of the story.

"You know, when Francesco started to undress to go swimming, I wanted to do the same. I had the strongest impulse to strip and take a plunge too. But something, I don't know what it was — some thing — stopped me."

"Thank God," I said. "Thank God for that."

I want to tell something about these tiny monsters. For they make the piranha seem like a nursery rhyme in comparison.

The candiru is unique in that it is the only vertebrate that will parasitize a human. The candiru is a

bloodsucker. They are eel-like in appearance and are about the size of a thin lead pencil. Their pleasure is to enter the human genital opening, either male or female, and then they worm their way up into the urethra where they open out their prickly spines on their gill covers and so imbed themselves.

They draw a great amount of blood from their victims. The principal problem for humans is that the candiru will reach the bladder and just stay there while the wretched host dies in excruciating pain. Indeed, there have been people for whom the agony was so great that they have slashed off their own penis.

I know of no death more horrible than this. I even say that an attack by a shark would be less frightful than that of the vampire entering one's genitals or anus and lodging itself to suck blood until it is bloated and satiated and its wretched victim has either screamed himself to death, has cut off his sexual organs in a frenzy of pain, or has died from shock and agony.

KILLER

And yet it is not really the great white shark, the octopus, the serpent, who excites our imagination to its limit, but the great monarch of the deep — the whale. The utterly fantastic leviathan. Of all animals it is the most difficult for us to understand. It is remote, gargantuan, it is totally mysterious. Above all, the whale is thrilling.

Who has not heard of Moby Dick? Who has not thrilled to the dark hunt of Captain Ahab and the attack of the great white whale when it smashed the *Pequod* and its crew to the bottom of the ocean, killing all hands with the sole exception of Ishmael?

Great whales have attacked men and boats since the beginning. Harpooners' boats have been taken in the very jaws of the mighty whale. Countless men have died hunting the mysterious leviathan.

There are two basic kinds of whales — those with teeth and those with a sort of screen or sieve in their mouths which is made of baleen or whalebone. This apparatus allows the whale to strain small organisms from the water as he feeds.

Toothed and baleen whales are the result of quite separate evolutionary steps. They evolved from different land animals many years ago and took to the sea quite independently of each other. Surprisingly, they are not considered to be closely related.

It is the baleen whales who are the leviathans; they make up the majority of what are called the great whales. For instance, the blue whale which reaches one hundred feet in length and weighs more than one hundred tons is a baleen whale. There are also the humpback and gray whales, and others. All the huge whales with the exception of the sperm whale are baleen whales.

Except for the mighty sperm whale all the toothed whales are small in comparison. Toothed whales are one of a large and varied group — including the beluga, or white whale; the narwhale, who has a twisted tusk; the little pilot whale; and the killer whale.

The killer whale, although by no means a small animal, is yet a good deal smaller than the great whales. But he makes up for it. He is ferocious and highly intelligent. Indeed, the killer whale often preys on other types of whale.

In the jaws of the killer whale sit forty teeth, each one at least three inches in length, and a good deal thicker. They are of ivory. Without the slightest doubt the killer whale is a fearless foe. *Orcinus orca,* **or grampus, is a tremendous predator.**

These swift and remorseless attackers hunt to-

Killer whale, Shamu *(UPI)*

gether. They hunt in packs, or pods, or a couple or three dozen — the mother, the young, and the bulls all together. The largest bulls can reach thirty feet and weigh more than ten thousand pounds. They are as ferocious as the shark and as intelligent as the dolphin.

It has been observed that packs of killer whales have a very complex structure of behavior. When hunting, the big bulls sometimes patrol near the shore while the smaller bulls and the young range in casual packs through the shallows, looking for prey.

When the killers attack a large whale it is a sight to behold. In assaulting a baleen, for example, they drive in from every direction, focusing their ferocious charges, however, on th e head and lips. When they have slashed through and ripped the lips, they expose the tongue which they then rip out and eat. Now and then, though, a big baleen will manage to win the battle, driving away the horde.

But killers prey on big animals. A killer whale has been seen to overcome a bull sea lion, and a pack will assault schools of giant tuna, tossing some of the fish which weigh 300 or more pounds, high up in the air. Seals take off when there are killer whales. In the stomach of one killer whale, who measured twenty-one feet, was found the remains of fourteen seals and a dozen porpoises.

Killer whales have a proclivity for attacking prey close to shore, especially other injured whales. In the *Journal of Mammology* C. Victor Morejohn of the Moss Landing Marine Laboratories in California

© Lorillard 1975

C'mon

Come for the filter. **You'll stay for the taste.**

Warning: The Surgeon General Has Determined That Cigarette Smoking Is Dangerous to Your Health.

16 mg. "tar," 1.0 mg. nicotine av. per cigarette, FTC Report Apr. '75.

©Lorillard 1975
Newport
Alive with pleasure!
Newport
20
CLASS A CIGARETTES
Newport
MENTHOL KINGS
17 mg. "tar", 1.2 mg. nicotine, av. per cigarette, FTC Report Apr. '75.
Warning: The Surgeon General Has Determined That Cigarette Smoking Is Dangerous to Your Health.

has described an attack by seven killer whales on three gray whales. Other attacks have been described of killers attacking gray whales.

Killers hunt a varied prey. They range far and wide. In the Antarctic they feed on penguins. One method they favor, upon sighting penguins on an ice floe, is a submarine attack where they will go under the ice, surface and throw their prey into the water.

There are a number of instances where killer whales have attacked ice floes on which there were humans. One of these incidents occured in January 1911 in the Antarctic; in McMurdo Sound to be precise.

The research vessel *Terra Nova,* commanded by Captain Robert F. Scott, had anchored by an ice floe. Herbert G. Ponting, photographer for the expedition, had gone out onto the ice and was photographing six killer whales that had surfaced not very far away.

All at once the ice under Ponting's feet heaved and began to break as the whales, acting in unison, submarined the floe in an attempt to break it and plunge Ponting into the water. Ponting was fortunate to escape to his ship.

It has been said that killer whales do not intentionally attack humans. But who knows for sure? In March 1952 a fourteen-foot boat with two men aboard was attacked by what was described as a killer whale about twenty-five miles off San Francisco. The men battled the beast with an oar and managed to escape, finally reaching shore. That it was a killer whale was disputed when biologists, later examining the marks left by the brute's teeth on the oar, decided it was a great white shark. But who knows?

Another instance took place when a crew from Marineland of the Pacific, out on a collecting expedition, roped a female killer whale. The whale let out a high-pitched alarm call, and instantly a big bull arrived on the scene. The two of them proceeded to charge the boat, but were killed by the crew.

During the 1960's killer whales became great attractions in a number of public aquariums. The first one to appear in an aquarium, and perhaps the most written about, was Moby Doll. This was in 1964. Moby Doll measured fifteen feet. She had been harpooned, the original intention being that she would become a display model. But the wound was not serious and so instead of being placed in a glass case, she was put into the Vancouver, British Columbia, Public Aquarium. But Moby Doll died in three months, presumably as a result of complications from the wound she had suffered. Interestingly, she was later discovered to be a male.

Other killer whales began to be exhibited to the public. Most of these were friendly, allowing their attendants to ride them, for example.

One case drew wide attention, however. This occured at Sea World, a public aquarium in San Diego, California, where newspapermen and TV newsmen were invited to witness a shapely young female trainer ride Shamu, a female killer whale, around the pool.

Instead of wearing the conventional rubber wetsuit the young lady appeared clad in a bikini, and climbed onto the whale's back just in front of its high dorsal fin. While the whale circled the pool her rider smiled and waved to the audience, apparently quite at ease. Everything was fine until she took a second trip around the pool. This time, alas, when the whale circled the pool it turned sharply, and its rider slipped into the water.

Instantly, the whale seized the girl's left leg in its great jaws and began to swim around the tank with the poor girl thrashing the water with her arms and screaming in absolute terror.

Fortunately, two scuba divers stationed at the side of the tank instantly slid into the water and swam to her assistance. As luck would have it, the whale had not submerged and so the girl managed to keep her head out of the water.

Attendants at the side of the pool held out long poles and finally the young lady managed to grab one. Assisted by the divers and attendants the girl got to the edge of the pool, but the whale, its huge head thrust out of the water, would not let go of her leg. Yet it appears that the whale was simply holding it for if it had wanted to, it could have ripped the leg off in an instant.

Finally, the divers, who were whale trainers, soothed the beast and it released the girl's leg, which had been cut, but apparently not too badly. Other similar instances have been recorded where a killer whale and its trainer have had a "misunderstanding"; but these have not ended in tragedy.

Edward R. Ricciutl has wisely pointed out that there is a great difficulty in comparing the behavior of an animal in captivity with its behavior in the wild, for captive behavior can be quite abnormal. He concludes that both in captivity and at sea the killer whale's attitude toward human beings is still an enigma.

However, there is no puzzle in the story related by Carl Fahnstock. Fahnstock was witness to one of the most awe-inspiring spectacles ever to take place in the waters where animals and humans meet. It was an event that brought tragedy to half a dozen families, death to most of the participants and near-madness to its survivors.

It is a story that has been doubted by some authorities. For there are no witnesses alive today, save the sole survivor, and because of the strange horror of what transpired certain investigators lean toward the explanation that Fahnstock was, and is, insane; and that therefore his story, never before written, is to be discounted. But of course there is the old truism that people believe what they want to believe; and so, perhaps, its opposite is also true — that people disbelieve what they want to disbelieve.

At any rate, here are the facts, as given by Carl Fahnstock, now an old man, who is no longer sure himself whether he is telling what actually happened or if it was just all an incredible nightmare.

It happened just at the beginning of the century. Carl Fahnstock, the son of a wealthy American financier, had signed on for a cruise with the *Star Rover*. The ship was a thirty-foot sailer with no wireless and no motor. Its skipper, Hardie

Cartwright, a Welshman, had had the idea, since developed and popularized on a much more lavish scale, of taking certain sons of the wealthy for a summer cruise on his yacht. For this the parents paid a healthy fee, and the boys, who were in their teens, were well served with adventure.

Along with the crew of half a dozen young men, Cartwright hired a couple of professional seamen "just in case," for his crew was usually green and had to be taught everything from the ground up, as it were, about handling a sea vessel. They would cruise the English Channel, the North Sea, and other points near England, which was the home base.

This particular summer, the *Star Rover* sailed from Falmouth down to Gibraltar, and then back on up north to Heligoland, after which they would return to port. They stopped at various ports, stayed ashore enjoying themsevles, fished, swam, and generally learned and enjoyed the great life of the sea.

Toward the end of July the *Star Rover* found itself in Scandinavian waters, up near Heligoland. For a day and night they had fought one of those always surprising but deadly storms that suddenly spring up over the North Sea. The ship had sprung a mild leak, nothing serious, but they were now sailing in slowly toward port to see about repairs.

Fahnstock, a rather good athlete in general, and an excellent swimmer, was in the water with two companions. It was a lovely day, and they had decided to take a dip over the side. The boat was moving along gently about five miles from shore and the swimmers were holding onto a line that was dropped off the stern of the boat. They often swam in this way, trawling themselves, as it were, when the boat was moving slowly but too quickly for them to swim unaided.

Fahnstock's companions, Jeff Miller and Hank Downs, were laughing and letting go of the rope and then swimming back to it, or letting it go and then catching it at the knot at the very end as the boat moved ahead.

Captain Cartwright, a man of about forty, had already cautioned them against letting go of the line, but they either didn't hear or didn't listen to him or just forgot.

Presently he called off the stern again that they should come aboard for he thought a wind might be starting up.

Just at that point a puff of wind did catch the *Star Rover* and drove it forward with a fresh impetus. The boys in the water shouted, and Fahnstock and Downs grabbed the rope. Miller grabbed at the line but missed and he was suddenly behind, swimming furiously to catch up. But the boat was gathering speed. Fahnstock and Downs yelled at him to get a move on.

Suddenly a shout went up from the deck of the boat. And Fahnstock saw the cook, William, who was a part of the professional crew, pointing to starboard. To his horror he now saw what looked like a fin cutting through the water. And then another fin. And a third.

"Whales!" the cry went up. "Come aboard!" And the boys on shipboard began pulling in the line with Fahnstock and Downs also pulling themselves along.

But meanwhile poor Miller had fallen farther behind. Fahnstock has described the fear he felt as he began pulling himself upon onto the boat, with many hands grabbing him.

"I kept thinking of poor Jeff Miller, and would the skipper put about. I was scared at the sight of those fins."

Both boys were safely aboard now, heaving from their exertions, and pretty well shaken.

"It's a whole pod of whales," the mate was saying. "Killers, I wager."

"All hands!" cried the captain. "We're coming about." Far to the stern now they could see young Miller valiantly struggling toward them.

"Can't we lower a boat?" someone said.

"We'll throw him a line when we come about," the captain said. "If we can get close enough. All hands!"

Meanwhile the pod of whales had knifed in closer. They were mostly invisible. All that could be seen were some of their backs and dorsal fins.

It was not so easy bringing a leaking ship about, but they managed; now they were bearing down on young Miller who had also seen the whales.

They were close.

"We'll never reach him," one of the horrified watchers said. "Don't we have a gun or something, maybe frighten them off."

It was just at this moment that another boy stepped out of the hatchway with a rifle he had brought with him on the trip, and before anyone could tell him not to, he had raised it and fired right into the wale pack. The mate grabbed the gun furiously and threw it back down the hatch. "You fool!" he cried. "You damn fool!"

And as they watched they saw the pack thrash with fury at one of them being hit. And now they were right on poor Miller whose screams clearly reached them.

"Stand by!" cried the captain. "Get to the rail to grab him. I'm steering right close!"

The rail was lined with eager hands to help the screaming boy back onto the boat.

"Grab him!" someone cried. "For God's sake, grab him!"

Hands reached over and Miller raised his arms. He was swiftly pulled aboard. Ah — but not before the jaws of a vicious brute had closed on his legs and severed them from his body. The great black and white killer whale fell back into the water with his booty, while the torso, arms and screaming head of young Jeff Miller were dragged aboard the *Star Rover*.

But they had no time to take this in. It was too great, too gruesome, too altogether revolting to their sense of sanity to see their shipmate — half of him — lying there on the deck, screaming to death.

And then, before they realized what happened, a great thud hit the boat. "I thought of an iceberg," Fahnstock later related. "But of course it wasn't."

It was the whale pack submarining the leaking vessel which was now going at a very slow speed due to its injury on the starboard side, and also the sudden lack of any wind.

Again the whales struck — as poor Jeff Miller screamed his last scream and died on the deck which was now flowing crimson with his blood.

Suddenly there was a cry from below and the mate came racing out on deck. "They've punched a hole in the starboard side where the leak is," he cried. "We're taking water."

"Man the pumps!" ordered the captain. "Someone — my God, someone cover Jeff Miller!"

Again the whales hit the wounded vessel and one of the boys was knocked down the hatchway where he badly cut his head and face. He came on deck covered with blood. The mate told him to go and bandage himself. There was no time for sympathy now. All hands were needed for survival, for the whales were leaping out of the water and snapping at the rigging with their great teeth.

The *Star Rover* was taking water heavily now. Some of the boys were fighting off the whales with oars and boat hooks at the rail. One young man — Charles Martining III — was all at once pulled overboard when one of the attackers caught his oar in his great jaws and Martining was either too frightened or unable to let go. In seconds the wretched boy was savaged down into the foaming pack of killer whales.

The holocaust continued for an hour, although Fahnstock couldn't really claim to know just how long. For it was — for him — a lifetime. The captain and mate had set off flares and raised distress signals in the hope that someone might come to their aid.

Now there was no wind at all and the *Star Rover*

was taking on much too much water. The whales had widened the hole in her side and the sea was rushing in. The boat was beginning to go down.

And then suddenly one of the grim attackers landed on deck. He had sprung from the water and there he was, in the very midst of them, his great jaws slashing, and his huge body hurling itself about the boat. In vain they fought him with oars and whatever else they could find. His furious fangs found the mate and tore him almost in shreds, and his flukes drove a boy over the side and into the sea where he was devoured.

Furiously, hysterically screaming, the remaining boys fought the beast in their midst. The brave captain drove a boat hook into its eye finally and presumably its brain, and killed it. But the damage the brute had wrought was appalling.

Now the *Star Rover* was foundering and it was only a matter of time before the pack of whales would simply swim aboard. In one final valiant effort the captain went into the sea, fighting one of the monsters with a marlin spike. Fahnstock saw him disappear. The remaining members of the *Star Rover* had climbed up onto the rigging and they clung there. But when the whales again hit the ship one of the boys was shaken loose from his perch and fell screaming into the jaws below.

The water now was over the deck railing and it was red and foaming. Only the mate remained now, with Fahnstock. Both of them clung to the rigging while the attackers swam through the *foundering vessel.*

"There!" cried the mate suddenly. "There!" He

did not dare let go with one arm to point. But Fahnstock saw the boat coming toward them.

He does not remember how they were actually rescued. He was told later that the crew of the rescue ship drove the whales off with harpoons. Fahnstock's hands had to be actually pried loose from the rigging, so terrified had he become that he was almost a part of the dying ship.

Strangely, a boy was found in the water unscathed. He must have been swept overboard and miraculously escaped the jaws of the attackers, or drowning. But he was quite out of his mind. While the mate, upon reaching the deck of the other vessel, **went totally berserk and had to be restrained.**

Carl Fahnstock is still alive. He is a very old man now. He has never written his story, nor will he. But sometimes he is not sure whether it really happened. He says that he is not certain whether he is telling of something that actually happened or whether he dreamed it. Could such a horrendous thing actually take place? Wasn't it really something he dreamed, a nightmare?

Who knows? At any rate, it is what Carl Fahnstock has told himself all these years; perhaps by telling himself it was a nightmare he was able to survive; perhaps this dark realm of dreams was the only place where he could bear the appalling memory of the holocaust off Heligoland.

DOWN THERE ON THE BOTTOM

Never had I known the taste of panic — not even when I'd been confronted by a hammerhead shark. I had been scared then, but nothing like this time. The attack by that moray eel was a horror I'll never forget. My body, my left arm and my neck certainly won't forget it. And it happened in the most beautiful place you could ever imagine.

You really don't have to travel far to find the real world of riches and beauty and infinite wonder. Sure, some people journey to the East, the Orient, to South America, or to the sophisticated art of Europe, the glory and grandeur of Egypt, Greece, and maybe even the ancient kingdom of the Khmers; but for me I simply drive a few miles from my home.

It's a half hour drive from my house to the shore. I live in southern Florida. Once at the shore I don my mask and diving gear and in just moments I slip into a world of unparalleled splendor, an unbelievable, wholly magical world. A mysterious world. The world of the coral reef.

Here, above the sandy plain of the reef's outer edge, I see a fish that walks on its fins and attracts prey with a lure dangling from its overhanging nose. Everything is here. I see garden eels, slender as pencils, curl into a vertical position looking like a group of question marks.

I see darting squid, jackknife. fish, barracudas, sharks, sea cucumbers, indigo parrot fish with teeth that have grown or evolved into birdlike beaks.

All the undulating rhythms of the water world are here to entice. The waving bottom grasses, the changing light and color, all add to the unbelievable life that is so constant — that is going on regardless of the fortunes of men with their wars and money and so called battle with nature.

And here too, in this underwater fairyland, I, the stranger, the intruder, am witness to the gliding sharks and barracudas, the groupers, the sinuous moray eel. It is a miraculous world — awesome, beautiful, timeless.

Coral reefs are among the oldest and richest animal communities on our planet. It is these qualities that have called me again and again to this underwater place of magic. What is the life there? What are the species that inhabit these fascinating "homes"? How do they live? How do they relate to one another? And even — yes — what am *I* doing down here?

I suppose I could be labeled a sort of marine biologist. But that's not my profession. I am a bank teller, actually, and I dive because diving is what I love to do. Not so much the actual diving, mind you — but the *seeing*.

One of my favorite spots, apart from the place near my home, is about four miles off the Florida Keys — Alligator Reef, a pile of submerged coral nearly a mile long. But for this, of course, I have to go by boat. I like to go with my wife and my son; sometimes we take along a friend or two.

Funny thing, I always knew that my wife was attractive, but it wasn't until quite recently that I found out she was also attractive to turtles. Equipped with swim fins and Aqualungs, my wife Mary, my son Joey, and I had been collecting angel fish in about eighty-five feet of water.

Suddenly an enormous loggerhead appeared, it seemed from nowhere, and just hovered there above my wife who, not seeing him, was busily filling her collecting bag. I'll bet he weighed a good quarter ton.

I thought he would move on, but he just stayed there, hovering, looking down at Mary. I figured he must have been attracted by her long hair which was flowing behind her.

As a rule, loggerheads are not aggressive. But rules are made, it is said, to be broken. And the loggerhead has powerful jaws and a tremendous potential for inflicting damage. With just one bite a loggerhead can crush a thick conch shell. I also remembered at that moment having heard of a fisherman who had been crippled by a loggerhead biting his leg.

Joey and I had our bangsticks with us, antishark guns that fire .357 magnum revolver cartridges. We kept the safety catches on as we moved toward the great turtle, poking it with our guns as spears. He paddled away. No trouble.

Except that hardly had Joey and I turned our attention to something else when the loggerhead was back. He was swimming directly above Mary, within six feet of her.

I shouted through my mask — and it is possible to hear that sound for a little distance underwater — and then I tapped my air tank with the bangstick to attract her attention. But Mary didn't notice. She went right on collecting specimens, blithely unaware of the giant turtle directly above her.

I felt a touch of alarm right then, but controlled it. Now Joey and I moved closer and shoved him with our guns — they were still on safety — really poking the creature; and we finally pushed him away. This time he stayed away. And I breathed a welcome sigh of relief.

Normally the great turtles swim alone, but I have come upon thousands of individuals of other species swimming together at Alligator Reef, and quite close by, what's more. Great masses of snappers and grunts will lie almost motionless, like great armies, waiting for dusk when they go their individual ways to feed.

The flamboyance of many reef fishes is astounding. This has three useful purposes: to confuse other animals, to assure concealment, or, conversely, to advertise the wearer's presence.

Grunts, for example, fishes with horizontal stripes, are adept at the use of confusion as a tactic of defense. When a marauding predator comes upon a milling school, with its shifting maze of lines, he has great difficulty in singling out an individual for a long enough time to zero in for the capture. Then, too, if the attacker dives right into the school without first selecting a single target, the fish have an excellent chance to escape by darting in different directions.

But there was a way to beat this, I saw. Large jacks first flash into the group of grunts and scatter them, after which it is easier to chase them separately.

A great number of the most beautiful reef fishes — for instance, the spotfin hogfish, the angelfish, the queen triggerfish — carry markings in hues that cover the whole spectrum. In most instances, their colors make them difficult to detect against the variegated background of the reefs, their markings serve to break up their size and shape and outline.

But if I'm to get to the point I had better stop digressing. A few years ago I began seriously to take up night diving. And it was on one of these dives that the thing I want to tell about happened.

My wife, my son and I had taken our boat out to a reef we'd already chosen. It was an extraordinary night. The tropic air seemed the perfect setting. High above the stars glittered like silver. But that is a poor description. We lay just to seaward of the outer edge of the deep reef.

It wasn't long before we were ready to dive. We had a lot of stuff — cameras, bangsticks, nets, spears, and signal flares — just in case we got far away from the boat. We wore Aqualungs and plastic football helmets on which were sealed-beam lights.

I climbed over the stern and, with my headlight on, dropped into the dark sea. Mary and Joey followed.

The three of us pulled ourselves hand over hand down the white anchor line, stopping every once in a while to relieve the pressure on our ears. Now at one hundred feet the darkness below opened up as the beams of our headlights touched along the pale ocean floor.

We landed on a plain of sand and coral rubble on which were a number of large sponges. A great colony of starfish made a carpet directly ahead of us as they waved their tissuelike arms while they fished for food.

Kicking our flippers we edged along the bottom. Now silvery clouds of reef herring swirled about us. Over on my left I watched a swimming crab holding a struggling herring in its pincers while devouring it tail first.

Reef life is fascinating; and it is even more fascinating when you understand how the reef proliferates. Coral, which is the real backbone of a reef community, looks dead, yet it is in actual fact a living animal. Indeed, its stony skeleton is like the shells of snails, or our own bones.

Those animals that manufacture the coral rocks are related to the flowerlike sea anemones and watery jellyfishes which, even in cooler climates, may be seen along the seashore.

There are corals living in all the oceans, but it is only in tropical seas that they form reefs. Furthermore, it is impossible for them to build reefs if the temperature of the water falls below sixty-eight degrees Fahrenheit for any length of time.

While the corals build, nature's destructive forces tear down. Numerous and varied boring organisms penetrate the stony coral. Weakened, the whole structure crumbles. In the meantime, new coral cities grow on the seaward fringe and face of the reef, and on the eroded skeletons of what was there before.

Remnants of rotting reef would shortly be washed away were it not for the seaweeds, stony algae, sponges, and a host of other organisms cementing the fragments together. What results from all this is a porous limestone, honeycombed with tunnels, grottoes, caves of all sizes. The rock is riddled with little nooks and crannies, as well as big potholes filled with sand. And it is here that the residents of the reef keep house. And, too, it is why some of them — the moray, for instance — are so hard to see. Until you maybe step on him.

The most miniscule crevice or crack is a room for somebody. And moreover, the reef is occupied to capacity!

But I was alert when I began moving across the sea floor. I was mindful of the fact that larger fishes often occupy the coral ledges and caverns of the reef. And a good thing I was!

For here all at once, without the slightest warning, was an enormous jewfish. I suddenly found myself within three feet of him. He was at least two hundred pounds, maybe more. I raised my camera. The huge, still head filled the viewfinder as I got ready to trip the shutter.

Some pretty vivid thoughts raced into my mind

just at that point. The entire sea turtle I had found in the stomach of a jewfish a couple of years back; the diver who was engulfed head and shoulders by a jewfish he had tried to spear; another diver who was knocked absolutely out by a jewfish who rammed his diving helmet.

But this one posed for his pictures, seemingly not at all hostile. It didn't matter, though, because it wasn't the jewfish with whom I was going to have to contend — but the eight-foot, hundred pound monster I stepped on as I backed into a piece of reef, preparatory to surfacing.

And suddenly the thing was on me! I felt a stab of pain in my left hand and dropped my camera. And all at once I knew cold, icy fear. I moved back quickly and now the fear turned almost to something like terror for I saw where the bite had come from. The moray slid swiftly out of his reef lair and moved toward me.

Instantly I readied my spear and drove it at him. I felt it thonk into his tough, muscular body which was as thick as my arm. But the strike appeared now to be no more effective than a wasp sting, for to my complete surprise and untold horror the serpent was slithering down the spear shaft, coming right at me, his monstrously wicked-looking face eager for the attack.

For a moment I was paralyzed. Never have I seen such an ugly, evil face as that which slithered toward me now on the end of its slimy, sinuous body.

There was nothing for me to do but get out of there. I suddenly realized at that moment how

Stonefish (*New York Zoological Society Photo*)

alone I was. Where were Mary and Joey? Where was the boat? I dropped the spear and moray and fled.

But if I thought that was the end of the matter I was grievously mistaken. The monster was off the spear in a flash and after me! He was huge. I well knew the frightful damage he was easily capable of causing.

There are about twenty species of moray eeels. Their savagery is well known. In the daytime they lurk in rock or coral crevices with their blunt, ugly heads poking out to see what's going on. At night these horrendous serpents squirm out of their hiding places to hunt for fish or sometimes an octopus. I had evidently stepped on his nibs just as he was sallying forth.

An octopus will hide from a moray, using any available crevice. Often, though, the abode he has chosen proves to be his own coffin, because the relentless moray can slip his head into just about any place large enough to take an octopus. Then, all the moray has to do is seize a piece of the octopus's arm in its jaws and spin swiftly round and round until the meat is torn off. In this delightful manner the whole octopus is eventually consumed — piece by piece.

Small octopuses, however, essay to avoid being eaten by hugging the moray in their arms. But the wily moray is ahead of this caper. He simply sheds the octopus by tying his own tail into a knot and slipping his muscular body headfirst through the loop of the knot, in the process dislodging the octopus.

Some of this knowledge was in my mind as I fled my determined assailant. I had lost my direction now in a moment of fright — yes, panic — and was not at all sure where the boat lay.

Now he was on me! His slithery form closed in as he attacked my head. I threw up my arm to protect myself and felt a stab of pain as those terrible teeth slashed in. Again and again I tried to ward off my remorseless foe. At one point I managed to grab him just in back of his hideous head, but now he coiled his fantastically strong body around my neck. I found myself staring into the most repulsively evil face I had ever seen. Sheer terror all but paralyzed me, as with my free hand I tried to loosen his death grip on my neck.

At once I lost my footing and almost gave up my grip. But I held on, still managing to keep his furious fangs from slashing me again.

Now I could feel myself weakening. And suddenly I had lost him. My hand had loosened **and he was out of my grip. I saw his wicked head** only inches from my mask and again the awful pain hit me as he struck my neck. And then my shoulder...

The next thing I remember I was on the deck of the boat, wrapped in a blanket. Someone, maybe Mary, was giving me artificial respiration. They had found me just after the moray struck; had dispatched him with one shot of the bangstick and had brought me on board. I was in agony, vomiting, and very much in shock.

We raced to the nearest point of inhabited land, and then to the hospital. The surgeon worked on

Mooray Eel *(UPI)*

me for four hours. But I made it. Thanks to my wife and son.

But I shall never forget that wicked, hateful, wholly evil and relentless face as the moray moved in to deal me those last strokes.

Nor will my arm and shoulder forget. For I have never regained the agility I once had in that side of my body — nor the innocence I had enjoyed whenever I had swum in that paradise of reefs below the surface of the sea. For me now, a second moray can always be waiting for me.

THAR SHE BLOWS!

We may question the literalness of the story of Jonah and the whale. Indeed, few people accept the story as having actually happened. Yet, as far as the physical possibility of such a tale, there is no doubt whatever. Some whales, to be sure, have relatively small throats, but the throat of a sperm whale is large enough so that he can swallow objects twice as large as a man and indeed they have a number of times, during their violent death struggles, vomited into the bloody seas great pieces of squid which have measured five to fifteen feet..

The sperm whale is the only great whale with teeth. Moby Dick was, of course, a sperm whale.

No creature has ever been larger than the great whales. The dinosaurs of prehistoric times reached forty feet in length and weighed some fifty tons. A whale may weigh as much as one hundred tons and measure 110 feet in length.

The sperm whale is not the largest, but he is certainly the most dramatic. His natural food is the giant squid, a huge, boneless organism whose tentacles sometimes stretch thirty feet from its body mass, and who, it has been recorded, has more than once dragged a ship and crew to the bottom.

On one occasion one of those great arms was found in the mouth of a sperm whale, one end of it partly digested in the whale's stomach and the other end wrapped in coils in the whale's jaw.

Ah, he is a marvel, the whale! A big bull whale will sound down (dive) for an hour and a half, and he can dive three miles in twenty minutes. He will sometimes come up with his belly full of chunks of squid. But the sperm whale can resist a pressure of 200,000 tons; how does he adjust so swiftly to the change in pressure as he dives or comes surging to the surface and even clean out of the ocean, diving himself into the air with his giant flukes?

A diver rising even a hundred feet has to break his ascent into rests in order to avoid the dreaded bends. But a great sperm whale in just half a dozen minutes rushes through a column of water with such speed that his colossal body is hurled out of the ocean into an open atmosphere where the pressure is around fifteen pounds to the square inch.

It almost goes without saying that the whale has an incredible amount of blood. Old whaling men have told of the vast quantities of blood given up by a wounded leviathan.

The flukes (tail, which runs horizontally, not vertically) and jaws of whales are their most effective weapons of attack. That great horizontal tail can measure across its tips as much as twenty-four feet. This is the whale's only organ of propulsion and with amazing power it drives that huge body through the water.

It's a fantastic thing, that great tail. It can propel the great leviathan right out of the water; and it has often tossed whale boats into the air, killing or maiming their crews. "Stove" boats is a common line in the old whaling ship log books.

But it wasn't only the danger of stove boats that the crew of a whaler had to worry about. There was also the danger caused by a sudden movement of the whale when struck by the harpoon. Those tremendously powerful flukes, stimulated by the unexpected pain of the hurled harpoon, would drive the whale **forward** or into a sounding plunge the depth of which could not be foreseen. Often the harpoon line flew out of the boat in coils and would entangle the body of a whaleman in its loops, sometimes even cutting of a foot, a leg, or an arm.

Besides all this, the great and highly formidable jaw of the sperm whale receives frequent notice in log books. Here's part of an old accounting by a whaling captain:

> ...the whale had his eyes on us; for as soon as we dropped the oars, he milled short round, and came down on us. I had the iron in my hand, and when his snout came in fair dart, I let drive. You might as well have darted against a cotton-bale. The iron was

thrown right back; he brought his jaw up with a sharp snap, and just nicked the bow, putting a hole through the garboard-strake... .He met me again square, head on, and pushed the boat astern. We knew he would use his jaw if he ranged his nose beside the boat; but when he offered his "life" I put my lance in, and he answered by spouting thick blood.

The great bleeding was often a prime hazard — drenching the surrounding ocean, covering the whalers in thick crimson and momentarily blinding them.

From this out he was ugly enough. He did not count much on his flukes, but meant mischief with his jaw. So we sparred for time, when he rose under the stern, belly up, with his lower jaw standing at right angles with his body. He brought it down like the quick snap of a hound, cutting the boat in two, except on one gunwale. I had caught a glimpse of Welsh, the tub-oarsman, as he was squeezed in the clamping jaw; and the after-oarsman had his leg from the instep squeezed clean off.

The line fouled in the wreck, and the boat was carried right down, leaving only the oars to float us....

A tragic report exists from the journal of the *Java,* written by Joshua F. Beane in 1905:

> ...two schools of whales were seen about daylight, moving slowly to the southward. Forty or fifty cows and calves, three miles away, filled the air with their bushy spoutings...while right ahead a dozen bulls made regular soundings of twenty-two minutes as they worked slowly to leeward.
>
> We soon had the weather gauge of the larger whales and three boats went sliding over the glinting water in pursuit. In less than half an hour the mate was fast and hauled ahead to dispatch his prize. He was met more than half way by the infuriated cachalot, the boat being saved by an inch as the crew sprang to their oars in the nick of time. A moment later the third mate's boat, in attempting to fasten, was nearly capsized, the whale running his head against the port quarter and shoving her around so unceremoniously that she was nearly filled.
>
> After a short consultation these officers approached from different directions with the understanding that if one was attacked the other was to pitch in on the opposite side, and thus, between them, trust to get a lance in a vital spot. At the first stroke of the oars, the mighty brute whirled upon them, smashing the side of the mate's boat, then settled, leaving four men struggling in the water, while the other two were perched

upon the bottom of the capsized craft, one at either end.

Of this partial security they were quickly deprived: for, as the whale came to the surface, he took the boat in his immense jaws, biting her in two fairly in the middle, with no apparent effort. The mast and two oars drifting together, were also snapped in twain and then this ugly customer crunched the boat-keg as if it had been an egg shell.

Meantime the only uninjured boat, of which I was one of the fortunate crew, picked up all the men, save one, and he sank, feet first, into that blue until a mere speck, fathoms down, then disappeared forever.

The mate's other oarsman, a Portuguese boy, swam toward us, uttering frantic cries for help, and not a fathom behind him appeared a great, blue shark, taking his time as if sure of his victim....

The whale lay sogging in his own suds just the length of the big tub of line away, giving vent to his anger by threshing the sea into a foam and snapping his great jaw by the way of a challenge that we were somewhat slow to accept.

As quietly as possible the picked crew, with an extra man to pull the harpooner's oar, advanced to the attack, while we, with the line, hauled gently nearer. He heard them immediately and with a roll and a plunge, his flukes cutting the sea in a mighty sweep, he turned to meet them.

The crew, having had proof of the monster's power, turned their boat as upon a pivot and made her leap from the water with their vigorous strokes, but the whale was good for five fathoms to their one in the uneven race, and they had hardly settled down to business before he was upon them. His nose struck the boat fairly under the stern. It was lifted high in the air and plunged head first from sight.

Henry Astor, who was at the steering oar, made a flying trip through the air, over oars and paddles, and disappeared in the water far ahead. The boat came to the surface after what seemed minutes of breathless anxiety to us who awaited the outcome. Mr. Antoine was still standing in the bow, his bomb gun in hand, a sickly smile upon his face. The crew was clinging to the water-logged shell, while oars, paddles and whaling craft were drifting about them...With one boat fit for duty, we trimmed our sails for St. Augustine Bay, a small settlement inside the Mozambique Channel, leaving the angry cachalot master of the situation, guarding with watchful eye the destruction he had wrought, and demonstrating his feeling by leaping half out of the water, snapping his jaw and pounding the sea with his broad flukes in his crazy fury.

A notable instance of the whale proving victor over man.

These old records are useful reminders to we of a

more modern time; for we must not forget the power of the great whale. Bear in mind that as late as the 1920s men were chasing whales in sailing ships.

There are, of course, countless incidents of whales battling men, and occasionally winning. Classic is Herman Melville's *Moby Dick*. Perhaps, not so well known, is the actual, true incident from which some of Melville's story was taken. This had to do with the whaleship *Essex* which had an extraordinary and horrifying encounter with a sperm whale in the year 1819.

The first mate, Owen Chase, rendered a service to all of us by giving a published account in 1821. It has the unmistakable ring of authenticity in all its harrowing detail.

The *Essex* sailed for the Pacific on August 12, 1819. The war with England had been concluded just four years earlier and now the American whaling industry was beginning to show its metal in the world.

Chase, who was an intelligent man, kept notes throughout the entire appalling adventure — at least up until the time he began to lose his mind, along with the control of his fingers, as a consequence of terror and starvation.

After the voyage, when he and the other survivors had eaten food again for a few months and had perhaps forgotten the strange taste of human flesh and the memory and nightmares of that great sea devil, he began to write up his notes for publication.

It was an ill-fated voyage from the very beginning.

The intention was to spend two and a half years hunting whales from Nantucket to Cape Horn and into the Pacific. It was an able crew — there were twenty-one men aboard. The ship herself had just been completely overhauled and was considered sound and thoroughly seaworthy.

Just two days out the *Essex* ran into her first disaster. She was proceeding calmly enough through the waters of the Gulf Stream when, all of a sudden, the watch saw a squall of wind approaching.

There was nothing so alarming in this, except that it came from the southwest, gathering itself all at once into an unbelievable fury. It hit the ship about three points off the weather quarter, just as the helmsman was putting her away to run before it.

Instantly, the ship was toppled over onto her beam ends. Her yards went over into the water. One whaleboat was stove and two others were smashed completely. The galley was knocked down and every loose article was just gone. No man was lost, which was a wonder.

Luckily, the real violence of the squall was contained in its first thrust, and now it abated. The ship, which had been slapped right over on her side, gradually came to the wind and righted.

No one realized at the time how important the loss of those two whaleboats was to become; for they were to discover that the loss meant doom.

They spent a couple of days at the Azores, picking up fresh vegetables and some hogs, and then they made for Cape Horn. Owen Chase succinctly describes the situation as follows: "Heavy westerly gales and a tremendous sea held us off the Cape five weeks before we had got sufficiently to the westward to enable us to put away."

A month and a quarter of steady fighting with the sea and the cold and the wind off Cape Horn may have been a fitting prelude to the drama that followed.

It was on November 20 that a shoal of whales was seen off the lee bow. At the time, the weather (according to Owen Chase) was extremely fine and clear. It was about eight o'clock in the morning that the man at the masthead gave the time-honored cry, "There she blows!"

The ship was immediately put away, and now ran down in the direction of the quarry. When the *Essex* had got within half a mile of the place where the whales were seen, all but one of the boats were lowered, manned, and now started out in pursuit. Meanwhile, the ship was brought to the wind, and the main-topsail hove aback, to wait for the hunters.

Chase had the harpoon in the second boat, while the captain preceded him in the first. The whales had sounded, and as the men lay on their oars, waiting eagerly for a rising, a large whale suddenly breached close by the second boat; that is, the great mammal rose vertically from the water with a tremendous velocity, sufficient to project about three fourths of its length into the air before it fell on its side creating a mammoth avalanche of boiling water.

But Chase drove his iron home and the whale's

great flukes struck the edge of the boat amidships and stove a hold in her. Chase instantly cut the line with the boat hatchet and saved boat and crew from disaster as the whale swam with great speed to windward. Water poured into the boat and Chase ordered a man to stuff all the jackets into the hold and then start bailing as the rest pulled for the ship.

Meanwhile, the captain and the second mate, in the other two boats, continued the pursuit, and soon they struck another whale. They were now a considerable distance to leeward, so Chase, who was aboard ship now with his boat crew, went forward, braced around the mainyard, and put the ship off in a direction for them. The boat which had been stove was quickly hauled in, and after examining the hole, Chase realized that by nailing a piece of canvas over it, he could get her ready to join in a fresh pursuit in less time than it would take to lower the other remaining boat which belonged to the ship.

Forthwith he had the boat over and was in the act of nailing on the canvas when he suddenly observed a very large sperm whale about eighty-five feet in length, as near as he could judge it. The great mammal broke water about twenty rods off the weather bow of the ship, and was lying quietly, with his head toward the *Essex*. He spouted two or three times and then he disappeared.

Chase relates that in "less than two or three seconds" he came up again, but now closer, about the length of the ship away. And now he was making directly for the *Essex,* at the "rate of three knots," says Chase.

Owen Chase ordered the boy who stood at the helm to put it hard up, intending, so he reported later, to steer off and escape the whale's obvious intention to attack.

The ship responded slowly and the whale, coming down at full speed, struck with his head just forward of the fore chain. The vessel shuddered and everyone was thrown to the deck. "The shock was as violent as though we had struck a reef," wrote Chase.

Now Chase and the men aboard the *Essex* saw the whale moving slowly to leeward. "Suddenly he seemed to go into convulsions. He thrashed the water about him into a white foam and snapped his jaws in a furious rage and then crossed the bow of the ship to windward."

But the *Essex* had been severly damaged. Chase decided that the whale was gone and he instantly ordered several of the men to man the pumps while he made arrangements to embark should the ship settle too rapidly.

Perhaps what is most outstanding about the first mate's account is its understatement. Here, the ship is hit, and is taking on water, thousands of miles from nowhere, and he simply records that the men were manning the pumps while he made plans to embark in the available boats. Those old whalemen were doughty souls!

But now, suddenly, and to everyone's horror, a cry came from the lookout standing in the bow.

"Mister Chase — look — he is making for us again!"

It was a chilling moment as they saw a great spout of white water a hundred rods directly off their bow. The whale came for them now with his head half out of the water.

Chase yelled at the helmsman to hard up the wheel but the vessel had not managed to come around before the great leviathan rammed in the ship's bow right under the cathead. "He then sounded under the keel and passed off to windward. We saw no more of him."

Clearly the *Essex* was doomed, and they were three thousand miles from land. Chase and the men now worked in a frenzy of speed. There was no time to repair the boat which had been stove before the ship was attacked. Picking up a hatchet the mate hacked away the lashings of the spare whaleboat which lay on two spars above the quarterdeck.

The captain and second mate were out of sight, still chasing whales. Six men carried the spare boat to the waist of the ship. Meanwhile, the steward began collecting compasses, quadrants, whatever might be needed for navigation.

By the time they had got the boat to the waist the ship had filled with water and was going down on her beam ends. They were scarcely away two boats' lengths distant when the *Essex* fell over to windward and settled down to the water.

So completely had the great whale crushed the planks and heavy live oak timbers that the vessel was an unbelievable wreck within ten minutes. No one had been able to save anything except what they wore on their backs. In the little whaleboat the men stared in awe at the horrendous, totally unbelievable disaster that had befallen them — with the suddenness and irrevocability of grim death.

Clearly they were all doomed — twenty men on the Pacific Ocean in three light open boats, surrounded by whales, sharks, squid and who knew what other untold horrors!

Below the horizon, several miles beyond the view of Chase and his boat, the two other boats that had been hunting whales were towing a dead whale toward the ship at the time of its destruction.

Suddenly the boatsteerer in the captain's boat cried out, "Oh, my God, where is the ship?" It had disappeared from his sight as he stood looking at it and handling his steering oar. The men were filled with total horror as they realized what had happened.

The first boat to reach Chase was the captain's.

"My God, Mister Chase," the captain cried. "What has happened?"

"We have been stove by a whale," Chase answered him simply, and then told him what had happened.

"We must cut away her masts at once," the captain said, "and see if she will right herself. Our only hope of saving ourselves is to get food and water from the ship."

The order was soon followed, and the men did manage to secure some food and water from the destroyed *Essex*. But night was falling, and Chase related in his account how some of the men became "nauseated with fear." Finally, some of them slept in what had suddenly become a fearful and hideous world.

It has been said by various students of the whale that the sperm whale does not attack humans, but will kill by accident or in reaction to being attacked. This has certainly happened often enough, as we have cited at the beginning of this chapter. Yet here, in the account of the *Essex*, First Mate Owen Chase tells us that "...this whale seemed deliberately determined to take vengeance on the hunters who had molested three whales in his shoal; the madness of a bull and his cows."

And now the scene was set for one of the most extraordinary and horrifying adventures in all the history of the sea. A voyage of hell. Chase continues:

> At 12:30 we left the wreck of the *Essex* and at four o'clock we lost sight of her entirely...During the night the weather became extremely rugged, and the sea every now and then broke over us...We allotted our food and water to last sixty days, believing that on the course we were then lying we would average a degree a day and than in twenty-six days we would reach the region of variable winds. In thirty more days we would raise the coast of South America...

Three boats, one of them in poor condition, and twenty men.

But then on November 28 they were to discover that their bad luck had not run out. The boats with sails raised were about a ship's length from each other. It was about eleven at night that Owen Chase finally lay down to catch some sleep. He had just fallen asleep when someone awakened him to say that the captain was in trouble.

Chase rose, listening to the commotion coming from the captain's boat. There was a sort of crunching sound, men swearing, and the captain's voice: "My God, it's a whale!"

Chase instantly prepared to put about, and ran his boat to the captain's in time to see a great form with jaws open snapping at the boat. But it was a starless night and the extreme darkness made it difficult to see. The men in the captain's boat were shouting and trying to see where to strike their mysterious assailant.

Now those great jaws opened again and seized the bow of the captain's boat and almost severed it right off.

And then whoever or whatever it was, was gone!

The night was so dark that no one could tell the size of what had attacked them. But the captain, fearing for the boat, made preparations to transfer into Chase's and the second mate's boats in order to lighten his own, and by that means, plus constant bailing, to keep her above water until daylight would allow discovery of her damage, and they could repair it.

When daylight came they all lay to and repaired the broken boat. It was decided pretty unanimously that the night attacker had been a killer who had followed them for some distance and then had suddenly, without warning, seized the bow of the boat in its jaws. They had beaten him off, but he had attacked again, inflicting enough damage to scare the wits out of everyone, but luckily not hurting any of the crew.

And now a further horror struck them. Since leaving the wreck of the *Essex* they had eaten daily of their salt-water soaked provisions and now they began to experience the most violent thirst. The scant water allowance was not sufficient to satisfy their salt-saturated bodies and yet they did not dare increase their rations for fear the water supply would not last until they reached land. They had begun to wonder too whether the land they came upon would be inhabited by savages or some other hostile foe.

But it was from this day, or night, rather, of the killer whale that their sufferings began in earnest. Some of the men drank their own urine in the hope that this would slake their raging thirst, but matters for them only grew worse.

They had two turtles which they had taken from the ship and now it was decided to kill one to allay the wrenching hunger that was upon them.

"The men waited impatiently to suck the warm, flowing blood of the animal. A small fire was kindled in the shell of the turtle and after dividing the blood among those of us who felt disposed to drink it, we cooked the remainder, entrails and all, and enjoyed it. The stomachs of two or three revolted at the sight of the blood and refused to partake of it...."

Then continued on their course, losing each other, finding each other again, shipping water in storms and gales, bailing, repairing injured boats, suffering the hell of starvation and thirst. Until...

Until they were down to an ounce and a half of bread. By now some of the crew had died and been buried at sea. "...a terrible death appeared shortly to await us: hunger became violent and outrageous...our speech and reason were both considerably impaired...."

One man threw himself down in Chase's boat, determined simply to stay there until death mercifully took him. Presently the poor man went completely out of his senses, calling loudly for a napkin and water, and then lying stupidly and senselessly down in the boat again, closing his hollow eyes as if in death. After a while the crew saw that he had become speechless. They managed to get him onto a board, for they were all extremely weak, placed him on one of the seats of the boat, covered him, and left him to his fate. "He lay in the greatest pain and apparent misery, groaning piteously until four o'clock, when he died in the most horrid and frightful convulsions I ever witnessed."

The corpse was kept all night, and in the morning Chase's two companions — there had originally been five — began as a matter of course to dispose of it at sea. But now, after some reflection, Chase broached them on the subject that must have been touching all of them.

The provisions could not possibly last and hunger much sooner than later would drive them to the necessity of casting lots.

"It was without any objection agreed to, and we set to work as fast as we were able to prepare it so as to prevent its spoiling."

Carefully, the limbs were separated from the body and all the flesh cut from the bones, after which they opened the body, took out the heart, then closed it again by sewing it up as decently as they could, and finally sent it into the sea.

They began immediately to devour the heart and then ate sparingly of a few pieces of the flesh after which they hung the remainder, cut in thin strips, about the boat to dry in the sun. Then they made a fire and roasted some of it to serve them during the day.

The following morning they discovered that the flesh had become tainted and had turned a greenish color and so they decided to make a fire and cook it at once to prevent its becoming so putrid as to be inedible. In this way they managed, but it was now that Owen Chase relates how he began to wonder who would be next. For they would run out of food again...

But the horrors draw to an end. On the eighteenth of February, three months less two days after the attack by the great sperm whale, the survivors were picked up by the brig *Indian*.

On June 11, Owen Chase finally arrived back home in Nantucket in the whaleship *Eagle*. His family had given him up for lost. And Owen Chase humbly concludes his grim and austere narrative: "My unexpected appearance was welcomed with the most grateful obligations and acknowledgements to a beneficent Creator, who has guided me through darkness, trouble, and death, once more to the bosom of my country and friends."

Those who are familiar with *Moby Dick* — and

those who are not — will recognize the lineaments of the wicked tale. Though perhaps the tale told by Owen Chase is even more frightful — for it was a true one; the tale of the great whale who attacked and destroyed a whaling ship and caused the death and madness of nearly its entire crew.

THE ULTIMATE MONSTER

Somewhere — perhaps in some cove far from the accustomed path of man, in waters of **Stygian** darkness, or possibly miles below the surface of ocean or an impassive lake — lies a creature still unknown to mankind, but sometimes seen, in story and legend, by men.

For by no means have all the creatures of the deep been identified, although many things have been *seen* by observers who cannot be termed unreliable.

Sea serpents have been the center of legend and lore for centuries. There have simply been too many intelligent reports of these demons for them to be discounted out of hand. The fact that their existence cannot be "scientifically proven" means nothing. When some great slithering monster drags you to the bottom, or slices a whole ship in two, it matters not one whit whether "science" agrees to its existence.

No longer ago than 1964 an oceanographer "discovered" a fish in the Bahamas that was previously unknown to science. And in the 1950s a jellyfish of a kind also previously not known to science was discovered in the Indian ocean.

In 1938 a large fish weighing 125 pounds was discovered — lobe-finned, it was, much like those that appeared during the Devonian Period.

In 1959 a larval eel over six feet long was found by a research vessel off the Cape of Good Hope. Edward R. Ricciuti has pointed out that the normal counterpart of this creature would be an immature eel two or three inches long that, when adult, would grow to between three to five feet. How large then, he asks, is the adult stage of the six-foot larva? And he asks the question whether huge eels ninety feet long live in the depths.

The point is that here quite simply we have evidence (and there is much more, but we do not have space) that creatures of ancient lineage, great size and unknown to science can appear in the sea at just about any time. In short, we just really do not know what is down there.

Indeed, the story is known of Robert Menzies, a well-known oceanographer who, some twenty years ago, discovered that *something* rather enormous roves the Milne Edwards Deep off the west coast of South America. Dr. Menzies had baited a two-foot-long steel hook with a three-foot squid and lowered it. Something in those black waters tugged, took the bait and left that powerful hook badly bent.

A giant squid? A great shark? The monstrous parent of a six-foot larval eel? A Kraken? What?

In March, 1971, the magazine *Natural History* wrote up an incident that occurred in December 1896 on the beach near St. Augustine, Florida. The article described a sea creature of a hitherto unknown enormity that had been beached. It was — after much dispute — identified as an octopus. But an octopus of titanic proportions. Its body measured twenty-five feet in circumference, its weight was estimated at six tons, and its tentacles were, at the minimum, seventy-five feet long.

Specimens of the animal's tissue were examined and it was laboratory-proven that in fact this was octopus tissue. A six-ton octopus! What could be more frightful than this! Here, then, could be the sea monster of the legends; and here too could be the answer to many of the strange disappearances of ships at sea over the years.

The octopus and the squid are cephalopods — the word means "head-footed," referring to the arms, the tentacles and, in the case of the squid, that sprout from the head.

To be sure, most cephalopods are harmless. *Some.* Others are among the most dangerous creatures in existence. The most terrifying of all is the giant squid — *Architeuthis princeps.* His existence has been asserted by many seafarers since medieval times, but until the last century these stories failed to gain scientific favor.

The squid has eight arms plus two tentacles which extend beyond the arms and have paddlelike tips. The arms and also the tips of the tentacles are studded with cups or suckers.

A giant squid's arms can reach a good twelve feet

Giant Octopus *(UPI)*

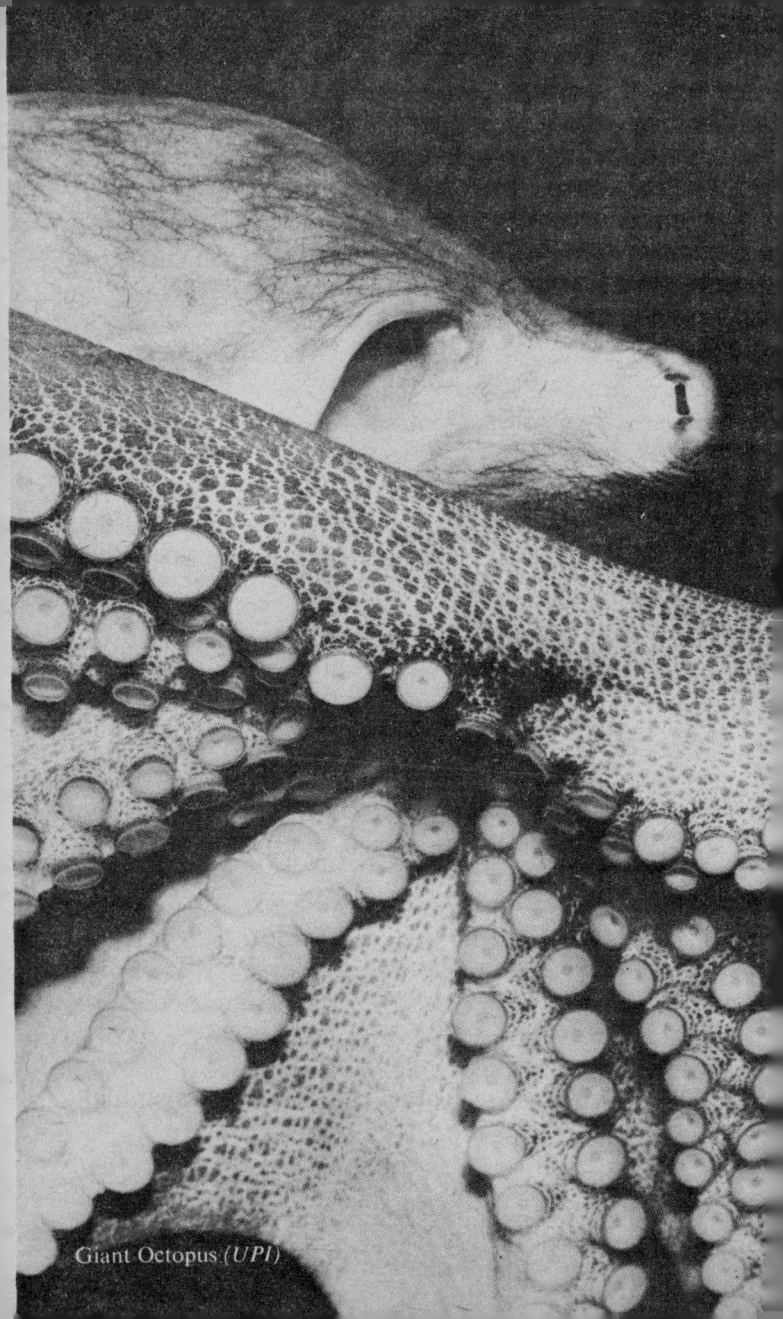

and the tentacles have a reach of fifty. In attack on its prey, the squid seizes the victim in its tentacles and draws it toward the embrace of the arms which then grip it so that the hooked beak of the creature can begin the devouring process.

The squid's beak is powerful. For instance, a Humboldt Current squid, not as big as the giant squid though all the same a ferocious creature, can bite chunks right out of a heavy wooden gaff. These demons with their strange, humanlike eyes complete with eyelids and iris and pupil, will swarm over bait thrown into the sea, hacking it with their revolting beaks, their eyes gleaming.

In the 1920s a squid about twelve feet long was thrown by a wave onto the ship *Caronia* during a gale in the Atlantic Ocean. The monster grabbed the ship's carpenter who would have been done for but for the help of his fellow crew members. Together they fought the brute with an iron bar for several minutes, finally vanquishing the thing.

An even more horrifying account relates that when the troopship *Britannia* was sunk during the Second World War, in March 1941, one of the survivors was clinging to a piece of wreckage when all at once a pair of tentacles were seen by some of his mates to appear out of the sea, and to pull him, screaming wildly, to his watery death.

While the name *'Kraken'* now refers only to the squid, formerly it was used to denote all sea monsters. It is thought that the monster Scylla in Homer's *Odyssey* was actually a giant sixty-foot squid.

Nobody used to believe that these beasts actually

lived. Sailors came home with fantastic tales of things "seen," but these were discounted as "tall tales," or as lore and legend.

But then in the second part of the nineteenth century a large number of giant squid were, for some strange reason, found floating dead on the sea, or stranded ashore. And it was then that the world began to accept the grim fact that these horrific beasts really did exist.

In October 1873 three fishermen in a small boat were attacked by a giant squid in a cove along the coast of Newfoundland. One of the fishermen had seen some sort of floating object in the sea and had unwisely poked it with the boat hook. The shape rose into a mass of terrifying arms and tentacles, gripped the boat and started to pull it down.

It would have done so, too, were it not for the swift action of a brave member of the party, a twelve-year-old boy who attacked the monster with an axe, hacking off one of its tremendous arms and a tentacle. The piece of tentacle that was cut off and that stayed in the boat measured nineteen feet.

Newspaper reports dated 1874 relate a horrifying confrontation with a giant squid. The steamer *Strathowen* was sailing from Colombo to Madras, and according to accounts it came within sight of a small schooner, the *Pearl,* which was becalmed on a smooth sea.

In a scene that must have been wholly terrifying, unbelievable, and unforgettable, before the bugging eyes of those on the *Strathowen* a gigantic squid rose from the smooth sea, slid its arms and tentacles around the *Pearl*, and pulled the schooner down into the depths.

The captain of the *Pearl* was saved and came aboard the steamer. Presently he told the story of what had led up to the attack by the squid.

While they were becalmed, they — himself and the crew — had witnessed a battle between a giant squid and a sperm whale. It may be remembered that the squid is the customary food for the sperm whale. In this case, however, there was a dispute over the whale's assumed perogative, and the two monsters of the deep tore at each other in vivid battle. They fell from view below the surface, but shortly after the captain related that he saw an enormous form of something or other rising out of the water. It was maybe half a mile distant. This turned out to be the apparently victorious squid who measured maybe 100 feet in length. It drew closer, and now the captain made the fatal mistake of firing at it with a rifle. Forthwith the great beast charged the *Pearl*, rammed it and dragged it beneath the surface of the water.

There have been countless sightings of sea monsters, giant squid, and other unaccountable monsters of the deep. In the early nineteenth century a number of monsters were sighted off the coast of Massachusetts. Notable was the famous monster that terrorized Gloucester harbor in August 1817.

Perhaps the most famous is the Loch Ness monster. Yet, other lochs have their monsters too. For hundreds of years the lochs of Scotland have been the seat of legends about water beasts.

To be sure, the lochs of Scotland are as perfect a

setting for these brutes as Transylvania is for Dracula. The lochs are unbelievably deep, and they are situated amongst harsh, mist-stroked hills. They are only slightly cut off from the ocean, which used to be in connection with these now-isolated lakes of water which lie in deep valleys.

The Loch Ness monster has been photographed, and even more interesting, sonar echoes picked up from moving objects deep in the loch indicate the presence of *something*.

Loch Morar also has a monster, who resembles the inhabitant of Loch Ness; and it has been seen — in 1948 by a boat full of tourists and in 1969 by two men who had a terrifying encounter while in their boat with a huge, humped animal with a reptilelike head and brown skin. One of the men hit the brute with an oar, which snapped. His companion fired a rifle bullet into their unwelcome visitor. Since then there have been a number of other sightings of the monster of Loch Morar.

All this, however, is only the prelude, the-setting-of-the-stage, as it were, for the story I wish to tell. I could, of course, write an entire book on sea monsters and on the giant squid in particular, for since the event I am to write about transpired I have researched the entire question very thoroughly.

Research, anyway, is my field — especially research into the past...

The interesting thing — to me, at any rate — is that not only have the legends, myths, lore, and *facts* about sea monsters recently been appearing in scientifically respectable quarters, but the question of the Lost Continent of Atlantis — another of my favorite subjects for research and questioning — has also come to the fore. And I mention this because it is as a result of my search for Atlantis that I have the following story to tell.

This hitherto "unacceptable" subject for so long relegated to the dusty areas of the occult and black magic and grade B films has at last been brought into the public eye, the scientific lens, the scrutiny of those publicly honored individuals who decide what is right and proper and, above all, useful for the rest of us to read and concern ourselves with.

No less respectable an organ than the *New York Times* carried, on July 19, 1967, a page-one story with the headline: A MINOAN CITY, FOUND AFTER 3,400 YEARS, IS LINKED TO ATLANTIS.

The newspaper then reported the discovery of an entire Minoan city buried by a volcanic eruption on the Greek Island of Thera in 1500 B.C. Dr. James Mavor, head of the expedition that was involved, announced that he was "satisfied that the discovery confirmed a theory that Thera was part of the lost continent of Atlantis."

Time magazine, *Newsweek,* and other periodicals gave much attention to the story. It was, indeed, the first time that prominent organs of the press had given credence to the lost continent.

Since then, of course, the subject of Atlantis, like the subject of sea monsters, visitors from outer space, and the life and "livingness" of all that had formerly been considered nonliving (plants, for example) has become subject for common parlance.

In any event, friends and I were eager to search for Atlantis ourselves. Others had tried before us, and many have tried since. But I venture to say that no one of them ever experienced the adventure we did. Or if they did, they did not live to tell about it.

Atlantis has been searched for in many parts of the globe — off Heligoland, in the Sahara, in the Mediterranean. But we decided we would search where Plato had said it was — off the Pillars of Hercules.

We reasoned that if Schliemann could find Troy, if Arthur Evans could find Knossos, and Henri Mouhot find Angkor, then why couldn't we find Atlantis?

Heinrich Schliemann had found Troy simply by reading Homer's *Odyssey*, which everyone had supposed to be only fiction. And so, we argued, why couldn't we find Atlantis by reading — *really* reading, studying — Plato's *Timaeus* and *Critias?*

Atlantis — that great island lying in the Atlantic Ocean! A beautiful land, rich beyond compare; its people wise, handsome, strong, living in peace and harmony with the whole universe; its all-wise rulers descended directly from the gods. Here, on this immortal isle, was the true beginning of everything that we know. Not 7,000 years ago in Mesopotamia did civilization begin, but 30,000 years ago on the lost continent of Atlantis.

So the legend tells us. Atlantis, the great continent that existed before the Flood, was split by earthquakes and swamped by tidal waves 12,000 years ago, and "in one terible day and night" sank into the ocean forever.

So complete, so terrible, was the disaster that history forgot. For some 10,000 years following the sinking of the continent — silence. At least, no written records of its existence have reached us. Yet evidence shows that the story — of fable, legend, myth — of a lost continent continued to exist. Although written records have not survived from that early period, a memory of something has been preserved.

But nobody wrote about it actually, until Plato. And he told the story in two of his works — *Timaeus* and *Critias*. And he said that it was located just west of Gibraltar in what is called the Sargasso Sea.

Later, there were others who supported his view; though critics claimed Plato was writing fiction and not a factual tale.

Our expedition was costly, to say the least; but we succeeded in acquiring the equipment we needed. There were six of us, all about the same age, in our middle and late thirties. We had laid our plans carefully. Two of us were Professors of Archaeology, one was an Oceanographer, two were English teachers, while I am a Journalist.

We were, I suppose, on looking back, a romantic group. That's to say, the adventurous type, as much interested in drawing attention to the *fact* of Atlantis as we were in actual scientific discovery.

We were concerned too — and wisely so — with the problem of sharks, whales, or any other sea animal who might cause us difficulties. We were all good swimmers, and two of us were highly competent divers, myself and Tom Merrill.

The Sargasso Sea lies roughly between the Azores and the West Indies. Its waters are comparatively calm, and yet considered impassable by ships in earlier times because of the amount of seaweed that lies on its surface.

According to Plato it is here that the continent sank, and all the seaweed and other matter floating on the surface of the ocean is simply what has risen from the lost land.

At the same time. Atlantis is said to have included the present day Azores and Canary Islands. The Azores lie off the coast of Portugal, about a third of the way between Europe and America. The Canaries are off the west coast of Africa.

According to many Atlantologists, including Professor Edward Hull, the Canaries and Azores were actually a part of Atlantis. The Canaries were at the southeastern end of the continent, while the Azores were at the northern end.

Accordingly, it was roughly in this area that we were planning to dive; off the Azores, possibly later off the Canaries.

It's funny how things happen; but I had been reading some old accounts of seafarers on our voyage to the Azores. We had hove to, just off a head of land, and were planning to make our first dive the following morning. I remember it was a beautiful night, the stars were almost more than the sky could hold and still be seen. There was more white than dark; or so it appeared to me. I lay on my bunk and read idly.

My book was an account by an old seaman. He

Giant Squid *(UPI)*

was talking about sperm whales, describing how they could attain a depth of a mile, for here was where their principal food lay, the squid.

The squid, this man was saying, is the greatest mystery of the deep water. "We don't know anything about it, only that it lives and nestles away deep, deep down about the roots and foundations of continents. And the wise Creator, before He launched the first sperm whale, sheathed him with thick blubber, and cushioned his brain-pan with junk and case, so that he could follow the squid to its deepest home."

Those lines caught me, especially the one that mentioned the squid way down about the roots and foundations of continents...

Next morning we were on deck early. There was no wind, the water was like glass, or, if you prefer, a great mirror for the sky. And the sky was absolutely clean. Not a cloud, not a bird. Nor any puff of wind.

Tom Merrill, my closest friend, was going down with me. Tom and I had dived together a lot. It is important to have a good "buddy" with you when you dive, especially in strange waters.

The others would remain on board. Each had his job, especially Jake, who would be on the lookout for sharks or any other unwelcome visitors.

We were in wetsuits and flippers, and had Aqualungs. We each carried a bangstick in case we ran into trouble with anything like a shark.

We had picked this particular place because, while it was not near what we thought would be the actual center of the continent (that being too deep for our regular diving) we thought some exploratory diving along the "edge," in shallower water might give us some necessary clues. We knew that when an island sank, as a rule its inhabitants climbed to the highest places, and since the Azores were said to be an actual remaining part of the sunken continent we might well discover something in the waters nearby.

I slipped over the stern and pulled myself down the anchor line, pausing now and then. It never does to rush when you're diving. You've got to let your body adjust. And this takes time. Tom was right behind me.

The water was warm, and the life down there was more or less what we had expected. We were actually looking for anything that might show us something in the way of flora or fauna, or rock formation.

We were just about to go back up when my eye caught something shiny just a few feet away. Thinking it might be a sea animal I poked it with my bangstick, which was on safety and so could be used as a spear. It was, I realized, a piece of metal. In fact, it looked a bit like an old coin. Anyhow I brought it to the surface and when we were aboard the ship we all examined it. It was apparently an old Greek coin.

"That's evidence," Bert Miller said. He was our captain and he was also a professor of archaeology.

"But what if someone just lost it there a couple of years ago," I said. And everyone laughed, because I had the reputation for being the group's great skeptic.

"I'm not kidding," I said. "Some coin collector could have lost it overboard. You remember about the vegetables on the oceanographic ship, don't you?"

I had brought that one up a number of times, to my own delight and to the dismay of whichever defender of orthodox science was conversing with me.

The story was that a research vessel exploring along the Puerto Rican trench had been trawling and had dragged in a basketful of various ocean fish amongst which were some green leaves that resembled vegetables. From this it was concluded that far below on the ocean bottom was an island, and moreover one with vegetation similar to our own on dry land. Until it was later discovered that just prior to the "catch" the ship's cook had thrown his garbage overboard. I generally used this bit of information to down anyone who tried swamping me on the subject of "science."

"Still it *is* an old coin," said Tom. "So why all the fuss?" Tom was a great peacemaker.

Next day it blew up a bit rough and we stayed aboard waiting for more favorable conditions. The day following we put out a little to sea and were soon at a point where we felt it would be profitable to dive.

It had been decided that Tom would take the first dive with me, but when we'd finished breakfast it developed that he had a slight attack of stomach cramp and so it was Bert who buddied with me.

It was again a clear sky and calm sea, and I was

glad. I have gone down in weather, but I prefer it like this. I waited while Bert got ready and then I stepped over the stern of the boat and started down the ladder. He followed.

It was dark. Nothing special, nothing out of the ordinary. I descended more, sliding through a school of some kind of fishes I didn't know, and then suddenly running into a lot of muck, seaweed I reckoned, since we were right on the edge of the Sargasso Sea.

As I look back now I wonder whatever made us pick this spot. It was deep, and there seemed not much that would be useful to our search. Still, a group of young adventurous men, looking for excitement and seriously interested in their search, well, we were apt to do anything.

Gradually, I don't know how it started, I began to have a strange feeling that I was alone. I cannot describe it, but it was eerie, and I felt a cold chill running down my spine. Where was Bert?

I was on the bottom now, and for an instant I felt the wish to be up in the boat. I looked around. I could see nothing. There was less seaweed visible, though some still floated by my mask. What I was looking for actually was any flora or fauna that would indicate the presence of land that had once been on the surface.

I had just decided that it was time for me to surface — still no Bert — when I saw what looked like a formation of some kind of earth or rock off to my left. I approached the mound, or whatever it was, when suddenly I saw two orbs staring at me, orbs or eyes with lids, eyes that gleamed in the most blood chilling way I had ever experienced. My blood froze all through my body. I have never been so terrified in my life. And it was then that I saw something, the creature — for it was a *creature.* Not a rock or a mound of earth from Atlantis — moving its arm or leg or whatever it was, sliding, slithering, and now snaking it toward me. . .and I was caught. It had wrapped its limb around my waist.

But fear charged my energy to the point where without even thinking I had my knife out and had slashed into that great arm of flesh and muscle, and for all I knew, venom too, and hacked at it and hacked at it until it released me — only to grab me a second later in still another embrace. It was the great squid's tentacle that gripped me now, drawing me along the bottom of the sea toward its waiting arms which would, I knew, suffocate me while its great hideous beak would devour me whole, with those eyes, those horrible, evil eyes watching.

I had forgotten my bangstick; but there it was in my hand. I slipped the safety and fired right into the monster's hideous face. And then with my knife I hacked wildly at its tentacle until again I was released. And here was Bert swimming toward me and now he too fired at the horrendous beast.

I shall never forget those moments of utter horror, as we raced to the surface. I could feel the monster's malevolent eyes on me and I was just waiting for the feel of those slimy tentacles and arms with their great suction cups, and then that frightful beak tearing and cutting and chewing at me, and the stench of its hellish breath which I could only imagine in my terror...

Eager hands pulled us aboard and it was while I gasped out what had happened that suddenly Bert Miller let out a scream and we saw the flash of the great tentacle, wet, enormous and overpowering, as it dragged him over the side.

Now in a frenzy we started the motor but it stalled. Then it caught. But here it was again — the monster. A tremendous thump and the little ship shuddered. Now the enormous tentacles slid swiftly over the deck and the great wet, shiny hump raised itself and I looked into those hateful eyes and I thought I would drop dead in my tracks with fear. Tom was shouting. He had fired his bangstick into the monster, but it was like throwing a pebble against a skyscraper.

"Dynamite!" I screamed. "Get the dynamite!" We had, thank God, brought along a box of dynamite.

I raced below deck as the boat careened in the brute's embrace. We were all doomed, I knew. In a wild dash I brought the box of dynamite to the deck, knowing we all had only seconds to live.

My God, I had never seen such an enormous thing in my life. It was the size of a ship; like a great mountain it rose from the seas, its titanic arms and tentacles already gripping our boat, its eyes glaring at us, its great back thrusting at Floyd, our navigator, whom it had caught in its iron grip.

"Right into him!" I cried. "Matches! For God's sake. give me a match!"

I had the caps off and now the ship shuddered and began to take water over its waist. I lit two sticks and then with all the strength I had, hurled them at that horrible spewing mouth...

I didn't stop. Tom had taken more dynamite and had done the same. Frank Filbin was hacking at one of the tentacles that was around the cabin, with an axe.

The explosion drove us almost overboard. And then a second explosion. Something smashed me in the face — like a great wave of mud. I realized then to my unspeakable horror that it was the creature's blood. Oh, it was thick and ruby red and it fell all over us and all over the boat like a great sauce. I was sick to my stomach, vomiting as I slithered on the deck which was covered with pieces of the slimy beast. And before my crazed eyes it began to sink back into the sea. In vain did I start forward, grabbing a boat axe to help poor Tom who was gripped by those massive arms. Too late. Screaming, he went over the side to his watery grave.

The ship was filling with water. The holocaust was more than we could tally at the moment, those of us who were left. Tom and Bert were gone, and so was Bill West. We were three now and we grabbed whatever we could to bail.

Suddenly as the great monster submerged completely there was a great roll in the sea, a sort of boiling, and pieces of what had once been that giant squid, that veritable beast of hell from the deep, rose to the surface. The water was crimson as far as I could see. And our boat was too — covered with the brute's blood, and our own...

We managed to stay afloat and we made it to shore. Those who met us could not believe what they saw; the carnage was like something out of a world war. Thank God we lived; although in shock for weeks, we still came out of it. My two friends Floyd and Frank are still around. But we never meet, and they don't meet each other. It is better maybe to be alone after such a happening. I don't know.

I only know that the nights are still sometimes long. And I sometimes still wish that I didn't have to go to sleep — and dream. I even wonder about mad people. At least they seem secure in their madness.

THE LAGOON OF TERROR PARADISE

You would think it was a South Seas tropical paradise with its lush, verdant islands, its flowing palms gently swaying in the blue trade winds, its placid waters mirroring the tranquility of a heavenly sky. This is the tiny archipelago of Truk lagoon.

Yes — Truk lagoon. And perhaps one remembers, if one is old enough, that some thirty years ago it was from this paradise that the Combined Fleet of Japan's Imperial Navy waged World War II.

The Japanese had taken control of the islands under the mandate of the League of Nations in the 1930s. As a result of this they began to develop a huge network of military bastions in the area.

Truk was prominent as a strategic base for naval operations in the Pacific. The deep lagoon was an ideal accommodation for submarines and big ships. Moreover, thousands of miles of ocean plus hundreds of out islands offered the perfect buffer since they were under Japanese control.

It was ideal in yet another way; the larger islands

inside the reef were first-rate base support airfields, harbors, and they even furnished underground storage. Finally, there was a great, encircling reef which had but four passages and which could handle battleships. And these passages were simple to mine.

This bristling fist of military power was indeed — it appeared — impregnable. From enemy naval gunfire this "Gibraltar of the Pacific" was unassailable. But airpower was another matter. First the outer islands behind fell as the Americans drove across the Marshalls, the Gilberts, the Marianas, and the buffer upon which the Japanese had counted vanished. Truk stood naked.

The hour of reckoning came on February 17 and 18, 1944 as U.S. aircraft from carrier forces ninety miles away from Truk swept across the great reef at dawn for a massive strike at all airfields and ships lying at anchor, and any other installations. The raid last for two days and is considered one of the most devastating of the Pacific war.

The planes were armed with torpedoes and 500- and 1,000-pound bombs. They succeeded in sinking more than half of the sixty warships, plus they destroyed 250 out of 365 planes, besides other massive damage wreaked upon installations, to say nothing of enemy personnel. Further attacks were mounted against Truk right through to the end of the war and the stronghold was finally surrendered. It became a U. S. Trust Territory.

Truk lay off the path of world traffic and so was more or less forgotten in the ensuing years. But below the surface of the placid waters of Truk lagoon lay those great ships and planes and other artifacts of destruction that had once been the pride of the Japanese Empire.

The bottom now held the giant warships, the merchant vessels still laden with cargo, bomber and fighter planes, even a submarine. In short, here was — and still is — a vast and wholly unique underwater museum.

And what is more, the effects of nature and time on this great fleet that has been preserved in its watery tomb in such an interesting way have created a strange phenomenon; for the artifacts are covered with an eerie shroud of remarkable marine growth.

Until the latter 1960s this strange place had been simply wrapped in oblivion; but then an airline began regular service to the area. Presently, rumor and factual word of the amazing underwater scene began sifting out. By the early 1970s divers began visiting Truk. And I was among them.

I suppose the whole thing was Robinson's idea. We were working for a film company specializing in underwater shots. And when we first heard about Truk it was Robbie who by real *chutzpah* got us the job of checking it out. Robbie was that way, he could talk his way into and out of anything. So the trip was arranged for us to visit the lagoon. This was in '74. We planned to spend about a month on the spot, exploring and photographing the wrecks.

I was anxious to go, but not as much as Robbie. I'd just met up with a new girlfriend and I wasn't too eager to be away from her for a whole month;

but Robbie insisted. Unfortunately, Croker, our boss, sent his son along with us — a snotty young man whom Robbie and I trusted as far as we would a pack of barracudas. I think Croker suspected Robbie's eagerness for the job, and was looking for some other motive. The old bastard always hated **parting with money, but he didn't mind free**loading his son on the company budget. Still, I looked forward to the trip. I love adventure, as the saying goes.

Our first day was spent with our guide in simply getting an overview of what was on hand. We took off in our launch on a lovely clear morning and moved swiftly over water as smooth as enamel. In no time at all we were over our first wreck.

We looked down on the ammunition ship, the name of which I couldn't make out even though the water was absolutely clear. We tried a few free dives just to explore and get the feel of things. Robbie's great. He just goes about his job and with no frills. But Crocker's son was something really out of it. I had begun to have an awful feeling that we'd have trouble with that young man sooner or later.

Anyhow, the three of us checked out the ship. It was eerie! Especially when we moved into the holds where the ammo and supplies were. Our flashlights lit on those stores when we entered the square opening of the forward hold. It was a real look into the past. I hadn't been in the Pacific Theater in those days, but in Europe. Still, looking at all that stuff gave me the strangest sort of feeling of nostalgia. Funny, because I'd hated every minute of the damn war when I was actually in it.

We checked around the outside of the ship too. It was in remarkably good condition. Much of her surfaces were overgrown heavily with coral and plant life, as well as a strange phantom covering of underwater cobwebs.

After we'd surfaced and rested a bit we made a deeper dive — with scuba this time — on a huge wreck. This was a prewar 10,000-ton luxury liner which had been converted to a troop transport. It was 500 feet in length, a titanic boat. While she lay in 110 feet of water, her beam was so great that, lying on her side, her port rail was less than 40 feet from the surface.

This was the *Rio de Janeiro Maru,* and we found her pretty much lacking in growths, and at the same time marvelously well preserved. She still had her enormous anchor chain extending off her bow and so presumably she had sunk while at anchor.

Later, we explored a gigantic aircraft carrier and some fighter planes. In the next few days we continued exploring, taking photographs and notes. Croker, we knew, wanted to make a feature film out of this sort of material. And there was plenty here.

The ships contained an inexhaustible amount and variety of things that one would need for supporting a combat force: telephones, typewriters, cooking utensils, medical equipment, tools, to say nothing of enormous amounts of still undischarged ammunition. I wondered what would happen if one day some of this was triggered.

We also found ambulances, trucks, and all sorts

of peripheral war equipment. The wrecks, it was clear, had developed into quite complex "reefs," artificial to be sure, but with all the reeflike attibutes, such as homes for underwater denizens. Corals, sponges, giant clams, small crustaceans, algae, sea squirts, sea grasses and anemones of various forms all lived here.

But we also saw tiny fish, the jacks, mackerel, tuna, large groupers, barracuda and an occasional shark. And, although we didn't know this until later, a whole conglomerate of venomous sea animals inhabited this strange world of coral and wreck.

But it isn't about the military lore and legend of Truk lagoon that I am concerned to write. I mention all that as background, as setting for the events I am about to relate. The events that occurred on our sixth afternoon at Truk transpired with such speed — and I must add, ferocity — that we were left breathless.

We were four again — Robbie, Croker junior, our guide Mano Popper and myself. Mano was an excellent diver and a good man all round.

Croker for some reason or other was not feeling well and in fact he was in a pretty foul mood as we motored out to the wreck we wanted to explore. Maybe he had a hangover, I don't know, but in any event he was abrupt and almost to the point of rudeness with Mano.

We had a rule that one of the party always remain on board; and it was Croker's turn. He said nothing, but I could see he didn't like the idea. He wanted to dive. But I told him he could go down later. One of the conditions Robbie and I had extracted from old man Croker when he foisted his surly son onto us was that he follow orders. The old buzzard was delighted, for he thought we "veterans of the deep" as he called us, would teach his son the "tricks of the trade."

The three of us slipped over the stern and slid down through the absolutely clear water of the lagoon. We were exploring a 300-foot *maru,* that is, a merchant vessel. It was pretty well overgrown with coral and sea grasses. Really weird looking with that thirty years' accumulation below the surface.

We checked out the holds and were going over the decks when I thought I saw a stranger-looking formation on the port side of the after deck. I wondered if maybe the *maru* had a deck gun or something like that. But then, as I was watching, not swimming but staying more or less where I was, I saw the shape move.

It was big. Huge. And then I realized with an unpleasantly cold shock that the "shape" was a giant grouper.

It really gave me a turn, for I'd forgotten about some of those underwater animals who are always lumped together with that silly phrase "dangers of the deep."

But *Epinephelus itajara* is no fish to forget about. Groupers and sea basses are no joke. They can easily take a man in those great jaws. This one looked to be a good thousand pounds.

It is a known fact that pearl divers in that part of the world fear big groupers more than they do sharks. And there are stories of the waterfront at

Barracuda *(UPI)*

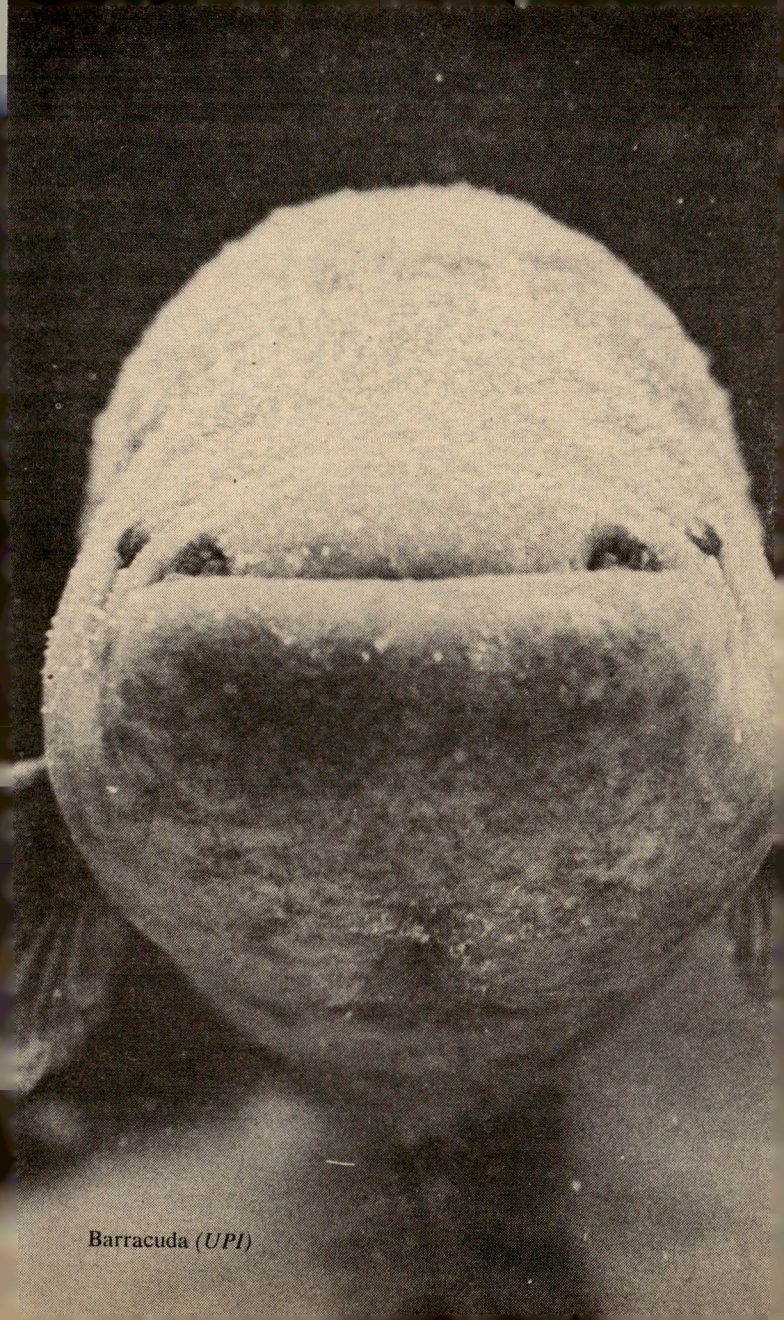

San Juan, Puerto Rico where giant groupers are said to lurk beneath the wharves to snatch youngsters who sometimes swim there.

In *The Living World of the Sea* William J. Cromie told how a pearl diver was swallowed by a giant sea bass just off the coast of Australia, but that he escaped through one of the fish's enormous gill openings.

I had heard too of a giant grouper once taking a naval diver into its enormous mouth. The diver, most fortunately, had on scuba gear which is all that saved him from being swallowed — the bulky air tanks being too much for his host to accommodate.

I was happy to see that the fellow I was watching seemed to want no part of me. I knew they liked old wrecks, making them their homes. And I was glad I had spotted him before accidentally bumping into him. I signaled Robbie and Mano, but they had already seen the giant.

I had just decided to swim over and explore the other side of the wreck when I saw a pair of flippers go by me. It was Croker. I was really mad. He was supposed to be up on board, waiting for us. I started toward him, signaling for him to surface, but he either didn't see me, or, more than likely, just ignored me. I was really sore.

It's no good — in fact, it's damned foolish — to lose your temper when you're all that way down on the bottom. So I just signaled Mano, who had also seen Croker, that I was going up.

But suddenly I realized that Mano and Robbie were pointing at something behind me. I turned,

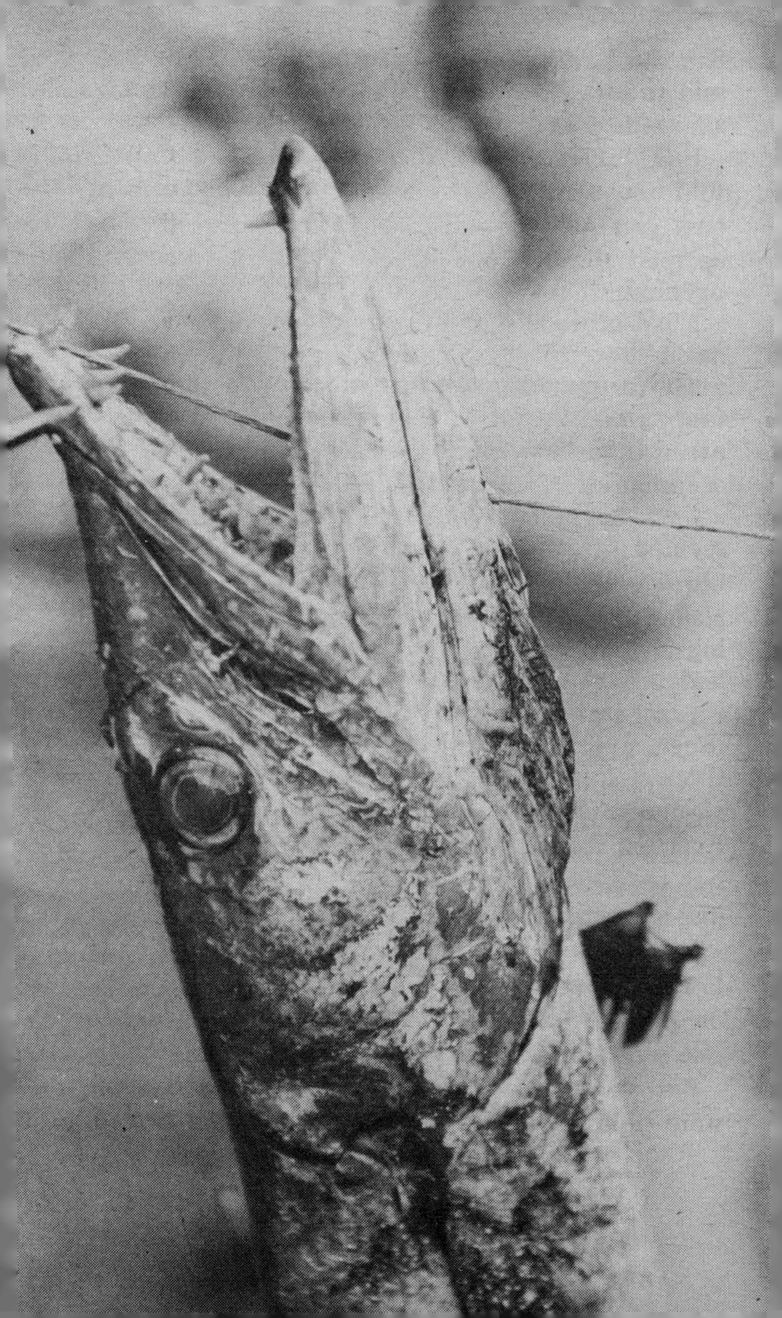

and instant fear ran up and down my spine. I can't help it, but whenever I saw them I would get that reaction. It was a great school of long, lean and deadly fish slicing through the water not very many feet away from me.

They were barracudas. The "wolf pack of the reefs" they have justly been called. These were not large, but they were as deadly as their bigger cousins, even if only about three feet in length. The point was, there were about a hundred of them.

The barracuda has been amply written up from way back. The great barracuda (*Sphyraena barracuda*) is the largest of some twenty species. At the most he is six feet in length and weighs around one hundred pounds. He was long, jutting jaws, mounted with thin, double-edged teeth. His body is slim; you can almost not see him at all when you face him straight on. He has the blood-chilling habit of vanishing, then appearing, then vanishing with fantastic silvery speed.

The noted authority on fish, Dr. L.L. Mowbray, has stated that the barracuda is without any doubt whatever the "most aggressive and voracious of marine fishes."

A writer in the seventeenth century, Lord de Rochefort, in his *Natural History of the Antilles* asserted that the barracuda "...When it has seen its prey...launches itself in fury, like a bloodthirsty dog, at the men it has seen in the water."

There have been notable attacks on record. In 1922 a young woman swimming off the beach in Florida was attacked by a barracuda and bled to death. Others were reported off the coast of Florida in 1947, 1952 and 1958.

But for me, at the moment, that silvery wolf pack flashing through those silent waters held a much more deadly menace. I was glad they were on their way someplace else.

But suddenly I saw something streak past me and strike into that pack of hunters. And I realized to my complete horror that it was Croker who had shot his speargun.

Furious, I signaled him to get out of there, and I saw that already Mano and Robbie were streaking toward the surface.

But the barracuda were swift as light. They had turned on their wounded or dead member — which was the only thing that gave us a chance. Mano and Robbie were on board when I broke the surface and their hands were great to feel on me as they pulled me up. I kept waiting to feel that terrible slashing on my legs, but I made it.

The three of us instantly grabbed Croker, who was right behind me, and pulled him up. And just in time, for those swift devourers were one split hair behind him. In fact, as he pulled over the side I saw the blood streaking down his leg.

It was a solid cut, but we had a first aid kit and managed to stop the bleeding. Then we headed for our hotel. It was one of those close shaves you like to tell about — or live to tell about.

But our adventure wasn't over. You'd think that would have been enough for someone like Croker. You'd think he would have learned his lesson and would now do what he was told. Wrong.

The very next day he learned the ultimate lesson. And it was not a pretty sight.

It was not something I feel glad he learned, I can tell you that. You know, sometimes when you don't like a person and something bad happens to him, you feel much worse because of your bad thoughts. Maybe it's like that with Croker. I mean, my feelings about him .

It started out all right. He was to stay on the boat because of his wound from the barracuda, which fortunately was not severe. We were damn lucky, is all I can say about that.

We had taken a new position now, and the weather was still beautiful. Croker seemed in better spirits, maybe all he really needed was to feel more a part of the group. I could see he was a lonely young man. With a father like old Croker you can't expect much.

We were down looking over some fighter planes. They were really strange-looking with all the growth on them, and the way the life down there had turned them into "reefs."

We got a lot of good pictures and I even began writing in my head some ideas for a script that I thought I could get Croker to okay.

Then around noontime we surfaced, climbed aboard and had lunch.

Croker really wanted to dive that afternoon. His leg wasn't bad at all, and he was really insistent.

I thought — well, why not. Let him, if he's that all-fired eager. So I said okay as far as I was concerned, and Robbie agreed. Mano was going to stay on board now, and the three of us got into our gear and slipped down below the surface.

The ship we were interested in now was the *Kyotono Maru*. It was an eighty-foot dive to get down into her holds, but we had heard there was a lot there. It was really like investigating a tomb, and I again had that real spooky feeling I'd had the first day. I turned and swam out of the hold, following Croker and Robbie.

Just out in lighter water I saw Croker moving toward what looked like a cabin hatch, but it was so overgrown I couldn't really tell. I started to turn away but suddenly something seemed to clutch at my guts and I swung my head back.

Too late! I saw the "hatch" move. Croker had his back turned, but he was looking away from me. I shouted almost bursting my lungs, but of course he couldn't hear. He had, I realized then, stupidly worn some bright metal on his wrist, a kind of bracelet some girl had given him. I could see its flash.

The giant grouper simply moved in like a dirigible and all at once Croker was struggling in that immense jaw, fighting furiously, as he was sucked off his balance.

I hurried toward him with my spear, and out of the side of my eye I saw Robbie sweeping in.

Croker had just about disappeared inside that titanic beast, his legs were protruding, and who knows where his head was.

I drove my spear as hard as I could into the grouper. He whirled furiously and the water was like a great whirlpool. Then Robbie hit him from the other side. The grouper started to rise. I had hold of one of Croker's legs now and was trying to pull. But I had nothing to brace against and was dragged along by the great 1,000 pound giant. Meanwhile, Robbie had come right beside me and taken hold of Croker's other leg and was pulling as much as he was able to.

But to no avail. We sailed along with the great fish as though we were a couple of handkerchiefs.

But then suddenly he turned, cutting back, and tore back the way we had come. Robbie and I were holding on to Croker, our bodies colliding with each other and with the underside and sides of that enormous monster.

All at once I felt something hit me and pain shot through my side. We had collided with the wrecked *maru*. I realized in a flash that the grouper was heading for its home, there to feast upon Croker and perhaps Robbie and myself as well.

I had dropped my spear, but Robbie's was still stuck in the grouper. Now I let go of Croker's leg and grabbed the spear. Because of the deck rail, I had a purchase and managed to remove it. And I struck as hard as I could right into that monstrous eye that was glaring at me.

Red flowed out and the giant fish thrashed about in a tremendous agony and rage. Again I struck. And again. And then I dropped the spear and grabbed Croker, and Robbie and I at last managed to pull him free. It was his tanks that had saved him from being totally swallowed.

Exhausted, terrified and frantic, we raced to the surface. Mano, who had witnessed the great disturbance below, was ready to pull us aboard. We were almost completely done in.

But poor Croker... His head and shoulders were totally crushed. He was unrecognizable. And of course he was dead. I have never in my life seen such a horrible sight as that partly digested man whom we had known only a few minutes earlier. He was now nothing but meat.

We looked at him. We looked at the great quantities of blood rising to the surface, thick as paint.

And we knew, both of us, deep in our hearts, that we were at a loss. As all men are in the face of great death. And we knew, too, that the sea is never safe.

THE RAVENOUS HORDE

From the majestic grandeur, the limitless beauty and awe of the ancient city of Machu Picchu to the desert of Paracas and then on to the border where Peru meets Paraguay is a long journey. For my wife and me it was a journey from Heaven to Hell.

It was Machu Picchu that had brought Ellen and me to Peru. Archeology is our hobby, and we're pretty good amateurs at it. Machu Picchu had long been a target of our investigation into the past — that fabulous city in the highest mountains where the ancient Incas had their final stronghold against the Spaniards; the "lost" city of mystery, rediscovered in 1911 by Hiram Bingham, and now about to be touted as a tourist attraction.

And it wasn't only Machu Picchu. Peru itself was a place we both loved. It is a truly beautiful country.

But it is also filled with terror. We shall never go back.

It happened five years ago. I have never written

any of this before. It is only by saying it, telling it — a catharsis, as the psychiatrists put it — that I may finally hope to resolve it.

Both Ellen and I had long been fascinated by the ancient Indian culture. Especially those cultures which preceded the Incas. The Incas were the last of the Indians in that part of the world but by no means representative of the highest form of its culture. Those that went before indicated that the Inca was in fact a decadent culture. But let me get back to my story.

I supposed it was Carlos who got it started. Carlos with his smile, his charm, and his knowledge of all the things that we were interested in. Yes, it was Carlos who told us about the tribe in the interior, over the border into Paraguay, who had never made peace with either the Incas, the Spaniards, or even the present rulers. They had kept their language and their culture through more than three hundred years of conquest.

We were seated on the verandah of the hotel at Paracas having delicious Pisco sours when Carlos told us about the tribe. We both rose instantly to the bait, and he laughed. He liked to tease us about our hobby, for he shared it himself.

"And we'll see piranhas," he said, smiling. "Americans always want to know about piranhas."

"They're the savage fish," Ellen said, "aren't they?"

Carlos shrugged. He was Latin and he really knew how to shrug with, as it is said, "eloquence." And then he went on to tell us something about these tiny fish.

Piranaha (*New York Zoological Society Photo*)

"I suppose, with the exception of the shark and maybe the octopus, no fish is so misunderstood and villified as the piranha." Carlos smiled reflectively.

"He's the one everyone depicts as stripping his **hapless victim to the bone even before he's submerged in the water.** One thinks of villainous mountain tribes tying up an enemy — or even better, leaving him untied — and tossing him into a river of piranhas."

"You mean to say it isn't true?" I demanded.

"It's true — and it's not true," Carlos answered. "A lot of the folklore on piranhas started through Theodore Roosevelt. How much he made out of that expedition into South America is fact and how much is fiction is a question."

I ordered another round of drinks and Carlos went on.

"Piranhas live in rivers in an area that takes in almost four million square miles of South America."

"That's a big bite," Ellen said. And then added, "No pun intended, please."

Carlos laughed. "It goes from the Atlantic coast to the eastern borders of Argentina, **Paraguay** and Uruguay. There are more than twenty kinds or species of piranha within this whole area. And most of them are harmless." He paused, lighting a small cigar. "The black piranha — he's known as *Serrasalmus rhombeus* — *is the largest. He and three other kinds of piranha are the ones that offer* a threat to people. *Serrasalmus nattereri* is the most dangerous." He put down his cigar and picked up his glass. "By the way, you know that the word *piranha* means 'tooth fish.' And let me tell you, that name suits him. He's got the most wicked-looking jawful of teeth you could ever find. And they're all sharp as razors. They are cannibals. They will even eat their own kind."

"You just said that they will strip an animal or a person right down to the bone," Ellen said. "Is it really true?"

Carlos nodded. "There was a movie film crew who once shot piranhas for a documentary as they absolutely stripped the flesh from a 400-pound hog which had been shot and lowered while it bled into the water."

A sort of a chill fell over the conversation at this point. And it was just this chill that returned to me — not in mental memory, but in actual fact — as the three of us now glided along the tiny lagoon in eastern Peru.

We had already fished a few of the species of piranha but only the mild ones. We had not yet run into any of the famous flesh-strippers. But now as Carlos mentioned how these toothy denizens of the rivers and lagoons can clip off a finger or toe, bone and all, with the neatness of a meat cleaver, I felt that old chill run through me. We caught a number of specimens, but better than this we met some of the Indians Carlos had told us about. They were friendly, but not obsequious by any means. When, through our interpreter, we asked about their culture, they were pleasantly impassive, as though to tell us it was not our business. When we asked about the piranhas they were more open.

Yes, there were piranhas. And some of the Indians even came forward to show scars where they had been bitten. They seemed quite casual about the whole thing, and for me, well, my fears were put to rest. I felt by now that the piranha thing had been grossly inflated and was no doubt largely the result of fiction writers and adventure-touts.

I should have known better. Somebody should have taken me and give me a slap across the face.

But, of course, hindsight is easy to come by. The extraordinary thing is how seldom we learn anything. Even when I witnessed the scene I am about to describe I still didn't get smart.

It was two days after we had spoken with the Indians. We had just pulled up in our jeep at an isolated lagoon in Paraguay's picturesque cattle country. Six or seven fishermen were setting a long net in the water. We watched them idly. I remember I was turning some ideas for pictures over in my mind.

In a sort of vague way I noticed, about two hundred yards downstream, a man and a boy approaching the water with a cow. The boy was leading the cow and the old man was following.

They stopped at the water's edge and now the man and boy sat down and began to eat what appeared to be their lunch. The cow stood idly by.

It was a simple tableau and I let my eyes fall on it without very much attention. We had just had our own lunch and I was feeling a bit drowsy as I settled down in the front seat of the jeep.

Ellen and Carlos were engaged in desultory conversation about the avalanche that had recently taken place in Peru. They were not looking at the cow who, I realized, had slipped her picket and had started into the water.

I must have dozed off. But I was brought rudely awake by the shouts that suddenly rose from the lagoon. I jumped in my seat and saw the fishermen racing out of the water. The old man and the boy were at the water's edge gesticulating and shouting.

And then I saw the cow. She was down in the water, but not covered completely, for it was shallow there. She lay on her side covered with blood and with what seemed a seething, frothing mass of something I couldn't figure out.

"The piranhas," cried Carlos as he came running to the jeep. "My God!"

And I caught it then, right in my guts, as I turned sick with horror. It was all over in minutes. The lagoon seemed to be filled completely with blood. And now it was the skeleton of the cow that lay in that crimson water. The piranhas had vanished. The lagoon was still.

We drove away in silence. So frightful, so sudden was the death of the cow that only later did I realize I had forgotten to put film in my camera. I had been snapping blanks, even while feeling nauseated by the sight of that ravenous, ghoulish horde. Today — all this time later — I'm frankly glad I didn't get any pictures.

But then, horrified as I was, I still was upset that I had not gotten it onto film. I considered going back and at least shooting what was left of the cow, but Ellen really didn't want to. And I gave in.

"I do want some pictures of piranhas, though," I

insisted. "After all, who's going to believe we saw all that if we come home with no evidence."

"Just don't go home with a couple of fingers missing," Carlos said, and he was quite serious. I realized that the scene with the piranhas and the cow had shaken him too.

Nobody knows how the *Rio das Mortes* got its name. The River of Death is a tributary of the **Araguaia** which runs through central Brazil. Carlos wasn't sure either.

"Some say because of a great killing," he told us. "Possibly a massacre of whites by the Indians. But others say it's because of the piranhas." He shrugged. "You still want to go?"

I could tell he wanted me to say no; and I will always remember that expression on his face, as he was just then, standing by the jeep. He really didn't want to go. It makes me wonder sometimes whether some of us might possibly be psychic, may know more than we think we know, in a different sort of nonthinking — sensing — way.

"Yes," I said to him. "I still want to go." Of course we were all thinking of the cow. But I was determined not to return home without some true photographs of those vicious little creatures. In fact — and I didn't mention this either to Ellen or Carlos — I had the idea to use some meat or blood for bait so that I could attract them and really catch them in action.

This time I was prepared with camera and film. I wanted no slipups, especially such a stupid thing as forgetting to load.

Our motor boat contained the three of us plus a native boatman and guide. It would be a four-hour trip upstream and Carlos guaranteed, as did the guide, that I would see the fiercest piranhas.

The sun was brilliant, high in the great sky, as we turned from the broad Araguaia onto the tributary with the compelling sinister name. The River of Death.

It was a slow-moving river, the water shined and it reflected the lush jungle on both banks. The tranquility was perfect and I wished we hadn't the boat's motor to disturb it.

Presently the river grew wide and we came upon a little group of thatched huts. We pulled ashore amidst barking dogs and welcoming Indians.

The Indians recognized our guide and called a special greeting to him. One of them, an old man, explained that the piranhas were harmless in this part of the river. He suggested that we go upriver another mile or so to a lagoon that was packed with really vicious piranhas. So we bid him goodbye and took to the river again.

Our guide, Tomas, had picked up a dead dog from the Indians, and half a goat carcass, which I gathered we would use for bait; at any rate, I had expressed my wish to photograph the scavengers in action. Again I checked my camera.

Now we moved out of the main part of the river and entered a shallow tributary. We cut the engine, paddled, and presently we came to a halt. A swamp lay between the tributary and the lagoon that the Indian had told us about. It was necessary for us to drag our boat over the swamp to the lagoon.

It was a small body of water, its surface covered with green muck. Tomas suggested we fish with hook and line for a while. It really looked like the right place for piranhas, I mean, in my imagination of course. I could just visualize them below the surface of the green slime. And sure enough, we were lucky right off, catching several of those toothy little beasts.

Now Tomas caught hold of an overhanging branch and tied a piece of rope to it. The other end of the rope he fastened around the dog, and then let it down into the water. We moved off so that we could see what happened.

Almost instantly the surface of the water broke, and the green muck moved as we saw a shimmering below the surface. We knew there was a furious activity down there. For maybe five minutes we watched and at last the movement of the water stopped. We paddled over and Tomas pulled up the rope with the dog. All that remained was bones. I felt my blood actually run cold; and looking at Ellen I saw all the color had drained from her face.

And so here were the really vicious piranhas. Elsewhere, to be sure, they were docile. What was the answer? Different members of the same general species? Or different conditions? I had to conclude that piranhas are like people, totally unpredictable. You just never know what the conditions are that will engender their ferocity.

"Let's put the goat in," I said. "And we can keep the boat close so I can get some shots."

"Didn't you get some already?"Carlos asked.

"Not that close."

The boatman headed us again toward the bank, and Tomas said, "We can hang the goat from the same branch."

"Let's go," Ellen said suddenly, and her voice was strained.

"I am for that," Carlos agreed.

And I said, "All right." Yet I was irritated with them, with their emotional reactions. After all, I had come thousands of miles and I wanted to get the most out of it.

Carlos had just moved to the stern of the boat and I was shifting my position to accomodate the new balance when he seemed to lose his footing. He slipped, at any rate, and he would have fallen overboard had not Tomas and I grabbed him instantly.

Carlos was white in the face as he thanked us. He was breathing heavily.

Then, as he sat down I suddenly saw to my unspeakable horror that in the melee to save him, the bottom of the little boat had been weakened by his heavy boots and water was suddenly leaking in.

Carlos saw it then. "Start the motor!" he said. Tomas and the boatman were already trying to do just that, for they too were aware of the situation.

I felt my heart stop as I listened to the fruitless efforts to get the outboard started.

"It has shorted," Tomas said. Again he wrapped the cord and pulled. And again nothing happened. And again...And then the boatman tried.

Meanwhile the rest of us were trying to bail out the water, using our hats, our hands, an old coffee can, anything. But there were five of us and the boat was taking in water fast.

Now Ellen bailed while Carlos and I took the paddles and started for shore.

We were shipping water fast now, and I was straining every muscle with the paddle, but the boat hardly moved. The motor was quite dead. Tomas suddenly picked up the goat carcass and heaved it as far as he could out into the lagoon.

"We will have to swim for it," he said. "Let them go for that. It will give us time."

Now the water was up to our knees. I didn't dare look back to see if the ghoulish inhabitants of the lagoon had taken the bait. But when I saw how far we were from shore I almost panicked. I almost *really* panicked. I looked at Ellen. She was still bailing, but the tears were running down her face.

Tomas's voice was even as a milled board as he said, "They have taken the goat. They are eating the goat."

"My God!" It was Carlos. He had stopped paddling.

We knew we had gained five, maybe seven minutes, provided there was not another group of ravenous fish beneath the surface. Or would those deadly gluttons be satiated for the moment and leave us alone?

"Swim for it," Carlos said. "We are making no headway."

And then, somehow, we were all in the water. We were swimming. Thank God, I thought, Ellen is a good swimmer. I stayed close to her, praying, struggling with the weight of my clothes. We were not far from shore.

And looking over at the bank I almost cried, for there were people, men moving about — Indians. I drove myself through the thick, slimy, terrifying water.

I saw Ellen being pulled up by the Indians. I was right behind her. One more stroke. I was on the bank. Gasping, crying holding Ellen who was shuddering and in a state of near hysteria.

And then I heard the screaming. Oh my God! It was Carlos. Carlos!

I knelt on the shore, too weak to stand, holding Ellen, along with Tomas and the boatman...

I could not drag my eyes away.

We watched. We watched the lagoon fill with blood and we listened to Carlos screaming. And we saw...

And then Carlos, our friend, stopped screaming. And the surface of the lagoon was once again still — as it had been when we first came.

THE GREAT LAND SHARK

There aren't many small country circuses around these days, but there does seem to be a sort of revival. People seem to be getting fed up with being so complicated and some of them are trying to get back to simple things here and there. Anyhow, the country circus under canvas — the big top — is having a renaissance.

The circus that traveled through Northrop County a few years ago had all the flavor of the oldtime affairs. It had a big **tent** with three rings, and other smaller tents with sideshows, games of skill and chance, things to eat and drink, palm reading, fortune telling with cards, and an assortment of freaks.

Every summer the circus traveled through the state, stopping at various towns and small villages for two or three days. And it was more often than not a sell out. There were the elephants and other wild animals, the aerial artists, the jugglers, bareback riders, and of course the clowns. It was a marvelous show, and a real professional performance. It was circus, not vaudville. Everyone had a terrific time.

Each year the circus featured a *Star Attraction.* This would be a special act or an exhibit — a strong man, a group of trapeze artists or tumblers, or occasionally some unique animal from a distant and exotic land.

This particular summer it was a large and wholly exciting creature in a great cage. Its name was *Crocodylus porosus,* the **estuarine** or salt water crocodile. He had been captured, so the announcer informed the gaping crowd, on an island shore off the coast of New Guinea.

He really looked prehistoric, with his scaly movements, his savage-looking teeth. Raw meat was tossed into his cage and the crowd watched enthralled, as the great beast fanged down the hunks of beef with his razor-sharp teeth.

"Ladies and gentlemen," said the announcer, a tall man in a dress suit, top hat and tails. "This marvelous crocodile, the fiercest of the fierce, this savage denizen of the South Pacific jungles, would think nothing of eating one of us right now for his dinner. Indeed, he has been known to eat an entire human being at one meal!"

The crowd gasped in awe and stared at the malevolent eyes behind the heavy steel bars.

The boys of the scout troop were especially excited as they crowded close to see, almost touching the edge of the great cage, leaning way over the wooden railing that had been put up to keep the crowd back. There were about a dozen boys and they were absolutely delighted with their own excitement. So, of course, were the other children, and there were a good number present. But the scouts were in uniform, and their leader, Mister Paulson, was almost as excited as they were.

He had to keep admonishing them not to lean over the railing, and for a moment they would move back. One of the boys was having even greater difficulty because he was trying to draw the crocodile on his sketch pad, and the crowd kept pushing him.

"The salt water crocodile has even competed with sharks for human prey off the beaches of New Guinea and other Pacific Islands," the announcer continued. "It is the largest and the most savage of crocodiles. In many places it is feared a great deal more than the great white shark!"

The announcer paused for this to sink in, and then he delivered his most thrilling morsel to the rapt onlookers.

"It is believed by some of the people who know these islands, by the experts, that one of these beasts — maybe even this crocodile right here before our very eyes — was responsible for the disappearance in 1961 of Michael Rockefeller, the son of Nelson Rockefeller."

A great thrill stroked through the crowd. The children chattered and chewed their gum and candy more quickly. The old people who were there tsked to themselves and each other. They could not take their eyes away. The great beast, with his hooded eyes gleaming, moved across the floor of his cage, poked his snout at the bars while one great fang curved over the side of his mouth. His big tail moved menacingly, as though he was pondering on what terrible thing to do next.

Now the announcer related an episode that occurred in the Pacific during World War II when about a thousand Japanese soldiers were under attack by British troops in a swamp on an island in the Bay of Bengal.

The Japanese wounded and their dead, lying in the swamp, attracted a number of salt water crocodiles to the scene. At night, when the shooting had ceased, the great beasts swarmed over the corpses, devouring them, and attacked the wounded who were unable to escape their ravenous hunger.

"And meanwhile, ladies and gentlemen, outside the swamp, the British troops could hear the pitiful, heart-rending screams of the beleaguered men inside that dark, savage swamp of hell! At the end of that terrible battle, only twenty Japanese were left alive — out of one thousand!"

He closed his peroration on a silence that was almost tangible.

"My God," said the scoutmaster, Mr. Paulson, to one of the boys standing near him.

Presently, printed cards were handed out which contained information pertaining to the estuarine.

"The crocodile," it informed the reader, "is the last of a long and ancient line that used to exist in the Mesozoic Era. This was when reptiles were the principle form of life on earth. The order began during the Triassic Period, some 180 million or more years ago. The crocodile, then, is a descendant of animals which formerly lived on the earth with the great dinosaurs. However, they managed to adapt so that unlike the dinosaurs they did not become extinct."

The show was over now and the crowd started to flow away. But slowly. Many were reluctant to leave their view of the great crocodile. The scouts wanted to stay longer, too. They were boys of nine and ten, and it was an especially exciting event for them. But Mr. Paulson said no. It was late afternoon, he pointed out, and they had to return to their camp.

The troop, as he called them, had pitched camp in a woods not far from the circus grounds. They were on a weekend outing. As a rule, Mr. Paulson had another man along for these expeditions, but the other man had fallen ill just before time to take off and so Paulson had proceeded on his own. Greg Paulson was an old hand with the boys, who liked him. They obeyed his discipline which was hard but not harsh, and usually reasonable.

"I wish we had brought our cameras," one of the boys said. "Couldn't we go back and get some pictures?"

His companions all voiced their agreement to this, but Greg Paulson told them there was no time, and besides, the show was over. This was the final performance and the circus would be knocking down and leaving for its next engagement.

The boys muttered, but they were an obedient lot. They returned to their campsite and cooked supper, sang some songs and listened to a couple of stories from Mr. Paulson. Then everyone turned in. It was about ten o'clock.

It was at a quarter after eleven — according to his testimony given the next day to the county coroner's office — when Mr. Paulson suddenly awakened. He had slept just about an hour and now, for some unaccountable reason, he had awakened fully. He felt, he said, uneasy. Was it something he had eaten? But their supper had been a simple affair. No...it was not his supper.

He tried to go back to sleep, but was unable to do so, for he found to his surprise that he was thinking about the circus crocodile. He rose, dressed, and went out to check the sleeping campers. To his dismay, he found that two of the boys were missing. Bobby Fuller and Harold Gonzales, who shared a tent, were nowhere about the campsite.

By now the other boys were awake and Paulson questioned them. Had Fuller and Gonzales gone into town to buy candy or sodas or something like that? Nobody seemed to know.

But now one of the boys made a suggestion that matched the concern that was rising in the scoutmaster's mind.

"Maybe they went back to the circus," he said.

And then another boy mentioned that Fuller had said he wanted to draw the crocodile for his history class. Fuller liked to draw; in fact, his father was a rather well known illustrator, and the boy, who was only ten, was talented.

"He was trying to draw him while we were there," one of the boys pointed out. "But he couldn't because everyone kept banging into him. I'll bet he went back to draw him."

"Why don't we go to the circus and look for them?" one of the boys suggested. Everyone took up this idea warmly, except the youngest two boys who were quite sleepy.

"You will stay here," their leader told them. "Guard the camp. And keep an eye out for Fuller and Gonzales should they return. They might not have gone back to the circus at all."

But he was sure they had, he told the Coroner's Court. He'd had that sneaky feeling too that something was wrong. And he
didn't want the other boys in on it. At any rate, he started out alone to the circus grounds.

In fifteen minutes he reached the road just above the field where the tents were being taken down. The entire place was lit up and there was a crowd gathered. Fear clutched him and when he heard the police sirens he broke into a run.

The first thing he heard from the crowd was that the crocodile had attacked his keeper while the man was trying to clean out his cage.

Then he saw the ambulance and the police, and the sheet-covered body on the stretcher and heard the cries of pain rising from the dying man.

"That animal is a killer for sure," someone said.

And Paulson related how he felt his blood run cold as he thought of the boys back at camp, and about Fuller and Gonzales.

He saw them then, standing by a big stack of packing cases which stood like a wall. They were in front of the crocodile's cage, which was partially covered with a tarpaulin. Circus hands were hooking the cage to a big truck.

Paulson had started toward the boys, angry now at having discovered their mischief, when a great scream rose from the crowd. And suddenly everyone started running wildly, it seemed in every direction.

It took Paulson some moments to realize what had happened. Somehow, to everyone's unspeakable horror, when the mangled body of the keeper had been taken from the crocodile, his cage had been left unlocked. And now, as the crowd screamed in a frenzy of terror, the great beast could be seen sliding from beneath the tarpaulin toward Fuller and Gonzales who stood with their backs against the high pile of crates, their faces ashen in the light thrown from car headlights...as the great reptile slithered toward them.

"Shoot him!" someone cried. "Run, boys!"

But the boys could not move. Paulson started to run, grabbing a milk crate as he did and throwing it at the crocodile. It smashed onto him, onto his back, and he turned, his jaws snapping furiously. Then, he slid closer to the boys who, still backed against the heavy crates, were totally unable to move and stood as though frozen in their shoes.

Suddenly a shot rang out and the crocodile twisted. It had been hit. But not mortally, for its great jaws now snapped in a speed that could not be recorded by the human eye as it seized Fuller by the leg and bit right through. The poor boy screamed in total terror as another shot rang out and police ran to close with the monster.

The beast slashed at his attackers as they were firing into him, severing the hand from one assailant, while poor Fuller lay screaming in a pool of his own blood.

Paulson had reached his side, and at the sight of what the great brute had done, he almost vomited. Poor Fuller was beyond help. He lay there screaming in pain and terror, his leg torn from his body, a great red cavity in his side. Meanwhile, the **police and keepers fired again at the murderous animal who in his final throes snatched three fingers from a keeper's hand, and sliced a long gath down the leg of a screaming policeman.**

The crowd, which had dispersed, now gathered again as though in a wink and stood in shaking bewilderment at the suddenness of the events while the brute, with those tremendous razor teeth, twitched and hurled itself about the ground, blood boiling from its mouth, which still held — to everybody's unspeakable horror — the white bone of an arm or leg.

The boy Fuller died on the way to the hospital. His friend Gonzales lay in shock for a week and then had to have extensive care for more than a year. The others recovered...more or less.

And Greg Paulson has spent the rest of his life with that horrendous memory of the great crocodile from so many thousands of miles away tearing and chewing and devouring while he thrashed in his death throes, taking with him a boy and a man, and wounding three others before the final fusillade of bullets put an end to him.

BEST SELLERS BY ROBERT E. HOWARD

THE SOWERS OF THE THUNDER (113; $1.75)
Four savage tales of sword and sorcery by the creator of CONAN. Special illustrated edition; first time in paperback.

TIGERS OF THE SEA (119; $1.50)
Cormac Mac Art roams the seas with his comrade-in-arms, Wulfhere the Skull-Splitter. Special illustrated edition; first time in paperback.

WORMS OF THE EARTH (126; $1.50)
The tales of Bran Mak Morn, King of the Picts, in a misty age of savage wars and ferocious resistance. Illustrated.

A GENT FROM BEAR CREEK (132; $1.50)
Larger than life, bolder than bold, Breckinridge Elkins is known as the terror of the Humbolt Mountains, where he does battle with grizzly bears, mountain cats, and a demon of a stallion called Cap'n Kidd.

THE VULTURES OF WHAPETON (144; $1.50)
Fantasy-adventure in a unique universe of jackals, vultures, wolves, monsters, buzzards — and men.

CORMAC MAC ART: SWORD OF THE GAEL (138; $1.50)
Cormac continued! Based on the mighty Robert E. Howard character, by another master craftsman of sword and sorcery.

THE INCREDIBLE ADVENTURES OF DENNIS DORGAN
(149; $1.50)
A mythical, magical foray into the inscrutable, indestructible Orient, where echoes of the hordes of Ghenghis Khan still send tremors through the land.

THE LOST VALLEY OF ISKANDER (157; $1.50)
One of Howard's greatest, found long after his death, is the story of the legendary warrior, El Borak.

Available wherever paperbacks are sold, or order direct from the Publisher. Send cover price plus 25¢ per copy for mailing and handling to Zebra Books, 380 Madison Avenue, New York, N.Y. 10017.
DO NOT SEND CASH!

ZEBRA BEST SELLERS

10½!
by Marc Stevens   (101, $1.75)

The brashest, cockiest star of X-rated films tells of his life and loves. Exclusive interviews with porn stars Georgina Spelvin, Tina Russell, Andrea True, and more.

THE WHOLE BEDROOM CATALOG
By Stephen Lewis   (131, $1.75)

Everything you always wanted to know about what comes in the mail in a plain brown wrapper. Produced by Al Goldstein, the most complete guide to mail order sex now available.

TRIANGLE OF THE LOST
by Warren Smith   (125, $1.75)

Startling new explanations for strange disappearances in The Bermuda Triangle.

THE SECRET FORCES OF THE PYRAMIDS
by Warren Smith   (114, $1.75)

Explores the mystifying relationship between pyramids and UFO's, ESP, Atlantis, space chariots, Edgar Cayce, and psychic energy!

WASHINGTON CALL GIRL
by Rachel Alciem as told to Richard Hofheimer   (121, $1.75)

A former Washington party girl reveals what really goes on when politicians and pentagonians start swinging.

THE SOWERS OF THE THUNDER
by Robert E. Howard   (113, $1.75)

Sword and sorcery, action and adventure, the creator of CONAN. Special illustrated edition.

Available wherever paperbacks are sold, or order direct from the publisher. Send cover price plus 25¢ per copy for mailing and handling to Zebra Books, 380 Madison Avenue, New York, N.Y. 10017. DO NOT SEND CASH!

GREAT WESTERNS FROM ZEBRA

BUFFALO SOLDIER by Zeke Carson　　　　(106; $1.25)

A renegade band of Apaches is relentlessly hunted by the U.S. Cavalry.

THE DEVIL'S TRAIL by K.R.G. Granger　　(118; $1.25)

A lusty, gripping tale of man against man and man against nature in a no man's land — the Old West.

DONOVAN by Max Kreisler　　　　　　　(147; $1.25)

The Apaches are on the warpath! They kidnap a young boy and hole up in the desert while they wait revenge on Donovan for murdering their chief.

THE VULTURES OF WHAPETON by Robert E. Howard
(144; $1.50)

A chilling foray into the unknown and mystical power that has turned men into jackals, wolves and vultures since the beginning of time.

A GENT FROM BEAR CREEK by Robert E. Howard
(132; $1.50)

Breckinridge Elkins, larger than life, bolder than bold, stronger than strong, does battle with grizzly bears, mountain cats, and a demon of a stallion called Cap'n Kidd.

Available wherever paperbacks are sold, or order direct from the Publisher. Send cover price plus 25¢ per copy for mailing and handling to Zebra Books, 380 Madison Avenue, New York, N.Y. 10017.
DO NOT SEND CASH!

SUPER SCIENCE FICTION, FANTASY, AND ADVENTURE

BIG BRAIN #1: THE AARDVARK AFFAIR
by Gary Brandner (108; $1.25)
Scientists at a top-secret research project suddenly go berserk — and Agency Zero calls on the high-level circuitry of Colin Garrett's BIG BRAIN!

BIG BRAIN #2: THE BEELZEBUB BUSINESS
by Gary Brandner (128; $1.25)
Can the Big Brain outsmart the Devil when Washington's chief foreign policy maker signs a pact with Satan?

DREAM LORDS #1: A PLAGUE OF NIGHTMARES
by Adrian Cole (111; $1.25)
Galad Sarian must penetrate the minds of the Dream Lords to uncover the origin of man.

THE DREAM LORDS: LORD OF NIGHTMARES
by Adrian Cole (148; $1.50)
Will Galad Sarian survive the vile tortures of the Dream Lords? Fantasy and horror in the tradition of H.P. Lovecraft.

FRANK MERRIWELL'S SEARCH by Burt L. Standish
(102; $1.50)
A secret ring with a hidden message leads Yale's greatest athlete on a merry chase. Long-time hero of millions of all generations.

FRANK MERRIWELL'S POWER by Burt L. Standish
(108; $1.25)
Frank Merriwell runs a race against time when a mysterious stranger schemes to ruin his name at Yale, to prevent him from being elected Captain of the football team!

THE COLOUR OUT OF SPACE by H.P. Lovecraft
(143; $1.25)
A world of dark horror and phantasmagoric fantasies. . . surreal beings and monstrous monsters created by the greatest name in the field of fantasy and science fiction.

Available wherever paperbacks are sold, or order direct from the Publisher. Send cover price plus 25¢ per copy for mailing and handling to Zebra Books, 380 Madison Avenue, New York, N.Y. 10017.
DO NOT SEND CASH!

SUSPENSE-FILLED THRILLERS

PEPPERONI HERO #1:
SANDWICHES ARE NOT MY BUSINESS by Bi
(10⁵

Pepperoni Hero plays poker for the biggest pot of his life and then tries to live to enjoy it.

PEPPERONI HERO #2:
PEANUT BUTTER & JELLY IS NOT FOR KIDS
by Bill Kelly (122; $1.25)

Hero faces a sudden death finish when he plays golf with the pros in Las Vegas's Desert Classic!

PEPPERONI HERO #3:
TUNA IS NOT FOR EATING by Bill Kelly (141; $1.25)

Pepper is almost jawed to death when a Great White Shark orders a Pepperoni Hero for lunch!

THE BIG APPLE by Symon Myles (135; $1.25)

Super sleuth Apples Carstairs goes to the pits before he gets to the core of the mystery that lands on his London doorstep late one night.

HOLLYWOOD HIT MAN by Van Saxon (123; $1.25)

Hollywood's top star makes her daughter take the rap when a mobster is stabbed!

Available wherever paperbacks are sold, or order direct from the Publisher. Send cover price plus 25¢ per copy for mailing and handling. to Zebra Books, 380 Madison Avenue, New York, N.Y. 10017.
DO NOT SEND CASH!